ESSEX MISCELLANY

Stan Jarvis

Ian Henry Publications

ISBN 0 86025 469 0

Printed by
Redwood Books
Kennet Way,Trowbridge, Wiltshire BA14 8RN
for
Ian Henry Publications, Ltd.
20 Park Drive, Romford, Essex RM1 4LH

FELSTED

Bamber Gascoigne in his *Encyclopædia of Britain* very neatly sums up for us the intention of William the Conqueror in putting in hand the Great Survey known popularly as the Domesday Book: "The written record of the survey of the land holdings in England, carried out for William the Conqueror during 1086 and summarised in this form in 1087 ... The main purpose of the survey was to ascertain the extent and taxable value of the king's lands and of land held as fiefs by his vassals, but it has also been of great historical importance as the first detailed account of England and the earliest record of many place names. It consists of two volumes: the Great Domesday, which is the summary of all but three of the counties; and the more detailed Little Domesday, consisting of the unabbreviated returns for Essex, Suffolk and Norfolk."

Those 'unabbreviated returns' list in great detail and in very obscure language all the classes of people in every town and village in Essex - all their fields, their windmills and watermills, their fisheries, their animals, even the number of beehives the villagers kept. All very serious and official you might say, but there is one entry in the Essex section of the Domesday Book which shows us that those Norman overlords were as fond of a joke as we are.

To appreciate their sense of humour you should first look in the telephone directory to confirm that there is a surname of Godsalve, Godsave or Godsafe. You will see half a dozen entries in most

The old watermill at Felsted

areas of a family name that goes all the way back to that Domesday Book. It sounds a very religious and holy name, but look under Felsted in that book and you will see that the manor, of some 480 acres was already in the hands of the church, the great abbey at Caen, but a further 120 acres had been given by King William to one of his naughty Norman knights, written down in that Domesday Book as 'Roger God-Save-The-Ladies' - for that is what the Latin in which it was written -`*dominus salvæt domina*' actually means. It is not surprising than that we can see he had quite a few descendants.

MOUNTNESSING

Thoby Priory is now a private house, less than a mile northwest of the windmill at Mountnessing. The reason for its unusual name is really quite simple - it was a priory so small that it was named after the first priest to be installed in 1141 A.D. Surnames as we now them had not then been invented and since he was known to all as just plain Toby the priest, and that was what it was called throughout the length of its existence.

Sad to say, though, there are only a couple of arches left to mark all that religious devotion, and in a less religious age a mansion had been built on the site. That house achieved its own fame. A hundred years ago it was described as `one of the oldest and most interesting mansions in Essex'. But those were the last days of the pride of that mansion and the glory of Thoby Priory for, on the night of Sunday, 13th August, 1893, it was the scene of a most horrendous fire.

At that time the mansion, owned by Mr. H. P. G. Blencowe, was the home of Col. A. C. Arkwright and his family. It was one of his boys, apparently, who inadvertently caused the catastrophe. He had been dressing for dinner by the light of a candle on the dressing table in the window. He forgot to snuff it out when he went down to dinner - a breeze blew the curtain across it and by nine o'clock that candle flame had become an inferno. That is when a servant spotted the weird light cast by the leaping flames in the upper room. A contrite young Arkwright leapt on a horse and galloped hard to Ingatestone, where the nearest horse-drawn fire engine was stationed. Imagine how, at that time of night, the firemen would have had to round up the horses from field and stable, back them into the shafts of the manual pump, harness them and urge them into a gallop. It was an hour before they arrived.

By then most of the roof had fallen in. It was not until half past one on Monday morning that the fire was finally damped down, and still the firemen stayed on, to prevent any possible flarings-up. It was all insured - no-one was killed or seriously injured, but Toby, in Heaven, must have looked down with much regret at the destruction of the last vestiges of his Priory.

COLCHESTER

The curse of the crooked cross was terrifying. If you mentioned it in the market at Colchester people would cross themselves and move away as quickly as possible. That was five hundred years ago. Brother Francis, a humble monk at St. Botolph's priory, did not give a fig for such superstition, for he had God on his side. When he was sent out to buy fish for the priors he went to the stall kept by old Alice. She had the best fish, even though everybody said she was a witch.

Brother Francis had been told to get the best bargain he could, so he tried to haggle with Alice, but she gave him short shrift, oblivious of the fact that he was a man of the cloth. They argued, tempers were lost, Francis called Alice an old

St Botolph's Priory, Colchester

witch. She retorted by screaming that she would put the curse of the crooked cross on his silly old bald head.

Francis laughed it off rather nervously and got his fish elsewhere. At evening prayers a brother asked him what was wrong with his head. His reaction was to put his hand to his head at once - and he felt bristles of hair sprouting from where it had not grown for twenty years; but it was growing only in two bands, crooked bands which made the sign of a cross. Francis collapsed in terror. The Prior was hurriedly called. He told Francis to wash his head in holy water and have the hair shaved off. But just as soon as they were shaved those hairs grew again in the sign of a crooked cross. There were some who said that the smell of brimstone overcame the efficacy of the holy water. So the monks tried exorcism before the whole priory. It worked - the hair shrivelled away under the solemn words of banishment. After the service they started growing again.

The Prior resorted to civil law and had old Alice examined by the Colchester magistrates. She, in her dotage, was very rude to them . They had her indicted for a witch immediately and condemned her to death at the stake. Before the dreadful burning could be carried out Alice had a fit and died on the spot. As soon as the news was known in the priory Brother Francis was shaved again - and he stayed totally bald. But I am sure of one thing: after that, Brother Francis was carefully polite in all his dealings in the market.

3

GREAT BADDOW

Some people don't like the sound of church bells, perhaps because their dings and dongs are not in tune with the popular music of these raucous times. In the days before discos and the inventions of Edison and Marconi church bells were the sound of music in every Essex village, telling everybody the time with their heralding of services in the day, festivals through the year and every night they rang the curfew - the time to cover the fire on the hearth and so lessen the chance of a disastrous fire spreading through the village.

The men who made these church bells had a great sense of the importance of their bells to a village. They founded them and tuned them as finely as they could, and when they finished a sweet-sounding bell they liked to engrave their initials on it, just like any artist proud of his work. Sometimes they went further than that and left a message engraved on the bell for those who would be ringing it centuries later. Had you the energy to climb up into the belfry of St. Mary's church at Great Baddow you would be surprised to see the inscription on some of its bells.

The treble bell is engraved, "I mean to make it understood that though I am little I am good." Another declares, "Whilst thus we join in cheerful sound may love and loyalty abound." A third tells: "To honour both of God and King our voices shall in consort ring." For all the bells another seems to sum it up: "The founder he hath played his part, that shows he's master of his art, so hang me well and ring me true and I will sound your praises due."

St. Mary's has nine bells - an unusual 'ring' you might say, but there are only eight bells in the belfry, the ninth hangs outside on the spire, under a little roof of its own. Beneath these bells, in this churchyard back in 1381 there gathered those desperate over-taxed working-class people who had come from all over Essex to make their protests heard, in what became known as the Peasants' Revolt. The men all marched down to Norsey Wood, Billericay, where they took up position against the King's soldiers, fully armed and armoured. The revolt was crushed.

TOLLESHUNT KNIGHTS

There something strange about Tolleshunt Knights. To start with, why such a grand name for such a small place? Probably because the land was leased from the King by one of his knights who in return would be ready to fight for him whenever the need might arise. Stranger still is the legend attached to Barn Hall, the big old farmhouse commanding an extensive view over Mersea Island and the sea beyond. It all started in Saxon days when a house of any size had a moat dug round it, to establish boundaries, to have water practically laid on, to deter thieves and to have a regular supply of fish. There is a long poem, author unknown, which starts with the digging of that moat and goes on to say how the builder:

... mustered his men on the morrow,
With plumb-bob, trowel and spade,
And brick after brick on the mortar

4

With faultless precision was laid,
And just as the long, stretching
    shadows
Were weaving the mantle of night,
The strong oaken beam for the rafters
Was fixed to the walls firm and tight."

Next morning the lord of Down Hall was dismayed to find all that work torn down. Who could such a thing? He set his men to mend the damage and stayed on the site throughout the night to keep watch. What a shock he got at midnight when the Devil himself materialised in a flash of fire and an odour of brimstone, all ready to rip the place apart again He saw the builder shrinking in the shadows - "Who's there?" he cried and the brave builder shouted, "God and myself!' and the mention of the Almighty's name frustrated the Devil's intended destruction. For three days the building went forward and for three nights the Devil was bested. But when the Devil made his challenge in the next night the weary builder shouted "Myself and God" - he put himself before his Maker and so his hold over the Devil was broken. The house was destroyed in a typhoon of terror and Satan tore out the builder's heart. He said he would have his soul as well, whether he was buried in the church or out of it. So the villagers buried his body in the wall of the church - and the Devil was beaten again!

William Kempster, of Orsett;
British quoits champion 1895,1896 and 1911

SPRINGFIELD

Quoits was once a popular game in every village in Essex, but now only the oldest inhabitants can remember it being played on the back lawn of the local up to the first world war and well beyond. It was essentially a strong man's game, played from time immemorial. In the fifteenth

century it was played with horseshoes, which gives a clue as to its origin. It has been suggested that the blacksmith's shop, the warmest place in the village, was always a gathering place for gossip and fun when a Saint's day gave welcome respite from the daily grind. Someone took a length of iron rod from the back of the forge, stuck it in the ground, then flung horseshoes at it, trying to get them to curl round the post without flying off again. There were plenty of young men to take up the challenge, and so `coits' or `quoits' was born.

It could be a very dangerous game. On St. Martin's Day, 1409, Christina Curley, nine years old, was hit on the head by a hard-flung quoit. At the inquest the villagers declared they could see her brain through the hole in her head. The carpenter who had thrown the quoit, which weighed over a pound, dashed down to the church and there prayed to St. Edmund that the girl might make a complete recovery. Miraculously she was healed, and what did she place on the saint's tomb in gratitude? The very quoit the carpenter had thrown.

The man who wrote out the rules of the game some two hundred years ago, was Joseph Strutt, an author and artist, who lived at one time in the Springfield watermill still to be seen in Victoria Road, Chelmsford. In his huge book on *The Sports and Pastimes of the People of England*, published in 1801, he tells us: "To play at this game, an iron pin, called a hob, is driven into the ground, within a few inches of the top; and at a distance of eighteen or more yards, a second pin of iron is also made fast in a similar manner; two or more persons divided into two equal parties which are to contend for victory stand at one of the iron marks and throw an equal number of quoits to the other, and the nearest of them to the hob are reckoned towards the game ..."

BRIGHTLINGSEA

What a lovely name for a place - Brightlingsea. It makes me think of the twinkling sea in the bright sunshine of a summer's holiday spent in a beach hut on the very brink of the water. How the sun shone and the sea sparkled that year! A `bright-ling' time we had beside the sea, so the place-name seems so appropriate. It was a bit of an anti-climax to find that the name comes from a Saxon called Brihtling who once ruled the roost in this area. It is disappointing too, to find that Cindery Island, the sandbank in Brightlingsea creek has nothing to do with fiery disasters - it comes from the Old English for `low-lying land.'

These names point to the early settlement of the place as a port at the mouth of the River Colne. The whole town was once an island in itself, shown clearly on a sixteenth century map.

Five hundred years ago there began in Brightlingsea an unusual and important Essex industry. Down by the Hard you walk along Copperas Road - that name is the last lingering clue to that industry. When Essex cloth-workers wanted a black dye (and they exported thousands of ells of black cloth to Portugal) they relied on the copperas gatherers. Black ink was made from the same stuff. Copperas occurs naturally in the clay on the northeast coast of Essex, as a twig-like nodule of bisulphate of iron. It was gathered mostly by women and children from the foot of the low cliffs where it had been washed out of the clay by the sea.

This copperas was turned into green vitriol, which today is still the basis of black dye. It was a dangerous process for the deadly sulphuric acid was a by-product. Men heaped up alternate layers of copperas and scrap iron in great piles. Then it was all dampened with water. The action of the open air was all that was needed to change it all into the two entities, vitriol and acid. The acid further reacted with the iron and so more vitriol was produced. Leaden tanks had to be used to resist its corrosion through the process of heating the whole mess to evaporate any remaining water.

The pollution it caused is demonstrated by the fact that the ground where it was produced at Walton-on-the-Naze became so polluted with the by-product of sulphur that absolutely nothing grew on the site for over a hundred years after the `factory' was closed.

RADWINTER

William Harrison lived in Radwinter, near Finchingfield. He went there as Rector and stayed for 34 years until his death in 1593. He should be remembered for two reasons. One is that he became famous far beyond the boundaries of Essex for his racy and controversial book called *A Description of England* and the other is that a lot of what he says seems to reflect our own view of life in England four hundred years later.

Living in the rough and tumble of the vigorous age of our first Queen Elizabeth, Harrison wrote about the evils of the time. He set out four major points on what he thought was wrong with the country at that time: 1. The need for greater discipline in the Church. 2. The importing of far too many goods to the detriment of British manufacturers. 3. Sunday trading is an intrusion into the long-established peace and rest and worship in this country. It should be transferred to a Wednesday. Fairs, markets and shops should be limited to six days a week trading. 4. Everybody who owned forty acres or more should be compelled to plant trees on at least one acre of land.

These are points which are being hotly debated in our own times.

Remember that he was writing in 1577 when he also says, "There are old men yet dwelling in the village where I remain who have noted three things to be marvellously altered in England within their sound remembrance." His language is too quaint and wordy to be reproduced exactly, but those three things are: 1. Many more chimneys have been built - showing that

The old school, now the village hall, Radwinter

even the poor wanted a fireplace where they could keep warm and hang a cooking pot. 2. Whereas these old men had been used to sleeping on a mattress stuffed with straw, with a 'good round log' for a pillow, the younger generation aimed at a flock mattress or even, would you believe it, a feather mattress and a proper pillow, reserved up till then for women in childbirth. 3. Village folk now setting up home were not content to use plates and bowls all made of wood, they wanted them of pewter if you please.

Whoever heard of such luxury, he wondered. Where was it all going to lead to? We know! Satellite TV, mobile 'phones, foreign holidays, etc., etc...

DANBURY

Have you ever wondered how Danbury Palace, that big house with its lovely lakes and walks and woodland got its name? We have to return to the days of Henry VIII, who reigned from 1509 to 1547. There was no house there then, it was all a deer park, belonging to St. Clere's Hall, on the other side of the main road. Henry granted it to William, the brother of his sixth wife, Katherine Parr. William became hard-pressed financially so he sold that park to Sir Walter Mildmay of the famous Chelmsford family at Moulsham Hall.

He it was who built the first house in the park and called it Danbury Place. It stayed in the family for a century, then, sold and sold again, it came to serve as no more than a farmhouse until, in 1831, it was bought by John Round. He had it completely demolished and had a big, new house designed by the famous architect Thomas Hopper put up in its place. When his wife died in 1845 he sold the new Danbury Place to the Church of England who had been looking for just such a residence for the Bishop of Rochester, in whose diocese Essex was then included. The Bishop added a beautiful chapel to his Palace, and The Palace it has been known as ever since even though the alteration of diocesan boundaries brought its sale into private hands in 1892.

A strange incident reported in the local paper in 1851 shows it was known as the Palace then for two "... impudent beggars ... were charged with begging in an impudent manner at Danbury Palace." They had dared to knock on the front door and were seen by the Bishop himself. He ordered them off the property, having seen right through their plea of poverty, but they persisted until they realised, despite their threats, that they would get nothing. So they ambled back down the drive followed by the Bishop and his servant, who had already gone for the police. The Danbury village constable took up the trail and followed them, unseen, all the way down to a house at Hanningfield, where they tried their begging tricks again. Now he had witnessed it himself he could arrest them and take them back to trial at Chelmsford. They were given free food and drink for a whole month - in Chelmsford prison - with hard labour.

There are a lot of London ladies who can claim to have had their babies in the Bishop's Palace. By 1937 the house, then known as Danbury Park, was being lived in by Brigadier-General John T. Wigan and his wife. Upon the outbreak of the Second World War the Wigans offered their house to the government for use as a hospital. The authorities accepted with alacrity and ordered that it should immediately be brought to a state of readiness as a maternity hospital.

There it was ready and waiting, but it was a complete surprise to the Wigans when, in the autumn of 1940, a coach load of very pregnant ladies, in the care of a couple of midwives, drew up outside the front door. They were the vanguard of a stream of expectant mothers brought up from the east end of London when the horrific bombing was at its worst. Mrs. Wigan and her helpers soon had them bedded down in the morning room. Soon this was reorganised as the recovery ward, with the labour ward and the delivery room upstairs throughout the war.

When the blitz eased off the London ladies stayed at home and 'expectant mums' came from the more local area as guests of the Wigans, having their babies and regaining their strength in walks around the beautiful, peaceful park and its lakes. Mrs. Wigan never called her house a maternity home - she said it was a family home, and her friendly helping hand reached out to every one of the mothers until they were fit to take their new baby back home.

On the occasion of the birth of the two thousandth baby the Queen of England visited Danbury Park and presented that baby with a complete layette. After that the mothers and staff presented Mrs. Wigan with a simple silver bowl inscribed with the charming message that it was given to her with love from two thousand babies. There must be a few of them still living in Essex.

Danbury Palace

10

BOREHAM

It is typical of us to call the old house at Boreham, 'New Hall'. It *was* new, back in 1517 when Henry VIII bought the estate and modernised the house on it to suit his requirements as a royal residence. He was there in 1524 with all his court to celebrate the important Feast of St. George. Imagine the crowd of retainers, grooms and servants who travelled in wagon trains from London to look after their lords and masters during their stay at Boreham. It was Henry who built the noble gatehouse with turrets which made up the south side of the great quadrangle. In 1538 Mary Tudor was there, sending Queen Jane Seymour presents of 'quails and cucumbs'.

Queen Elizabeth inherited New Hall and granted it to Thomas Ratcliffe, Earl of Sussex, in 1573, and that date incised on the wall of the west wing shows he made many changes. Then George Villiers, Duke of Buckingham, bought it in 1620 for something like three million pounds in today's money. It was bad luck that he was a Royalist, for the Parliamentarians took over the place, and let Oliver Cromwell buy it for the token price of just five shillings, or 25p.

We have proof of its age in John Evelyn's diary of 1656 "... I returned homeward passing through Colchester; and by the way neere the antient town of Chelmsford, saw New Hall, built in parke by Henry VII and VIII and given by Queen Elizabeth to the Earle of Sussex, who sold it to the late great Duke of Buckingham, and since seized by O. Cromwell (pretended Protector) ...

above all I admired the faire avenue planted with stately trees in 4 rowes for neere a mile in length ..."

Then another important man comes into the story. George Monck, Duke of Albemarle, was trusted by both sides in the Civil War and was able to arrange the return of the King in 1660. His reward was New Hall and a pension of £7,000 a year. Here he lived in retirement, breeding horses and keeping open house for titled visitors until he became ill and died of dropsy in 1670. His son, the second Duke, entertained James II here in May, 1686 - the last such royal visit to New Hall.

New Hall was being lived in by John Sheffield, 3rd Earl of Mulgrave and 1st Duke of Buckingham, at the end of the 17th century when he was commanded to go to Spain with the Prince of Wales. He had to leave behind his dear wife Katherine, daughter of Fulke Greville, 5th Lord Brooke, and their baby Mary, known affectionately as Moll. He adored them both and looked forward to any letter which might survive the sketchy postal service of the day. He was delighted to receive one which has survived for us to read today. How closely it brings that little family close to our hearts despite all our modern sophistication! It opens, "Dear Heart" and goes on to speak of the baby:

"She loves dancing extremely, and when the saraband is played she will get her thumb and finger together, offering to snap; and then when Tom Duff is sung she will shake her apron. She will be excellent as a hat, for if one lay her down she will kick her legs over her head; but when she is older I hope she will grow more modest.

Everybody says she grows every day more like you ... you shall have her picture very shortly. I am very glad you have the pearls, and that you like them so well; and am sure they do not help you to win the ladies' hearts.

"Yourself is a jewel that will win the hearts of all the women in the world; but I am confident it is not in their power to win your heart from a heart that is, was, and ever shall be yours till death ... When the King went to Newhall it was reported here in town that he went to meet you there; I would they had said truly."

The Duchess, while then staying at their town house, goes on to report all the work in hand to beautify the gardens at New Hall, then ends her letter:

"Thus hoping I have obeyed your commands in sending you word of all things you bade me I rest

Your most dutiful wife till death,

K.Buckingham"

It is sad to find that after four years of happy marriage she died, on 7th February, 1703/4.

The entrance to New Hall, Boreham, showing the royal arms and an inscription lauding Queen Elizabeth I

12

WOODHAM FERRERS

Edwin's Hall in Woodham Ferrers has passed through the hands of many owners since it was built around 1576, for the Archbishop of York, Edwin Sandys, whose family had owned the land from the beginning of the century. When he died he left his widow as the tenant for her life-time of both house and land, but some argument arose with a lessee of part of Edwin's Hall and at midnight in May, 1594, fourteen men armed with cudgels, swords and even 'guns charged with shot and powder' broke down doors and windows wounded three of Mistress Sandys' servants and drove the widow and her son out of the Hall. The lessee actually encouraged his gang to kill the old lady so that he could assert his right to the whole place. But she was saved and the gangsters were imprisoned. She lived on until 1610 and lies now in St. Mary's church under a charming and elaborate monument.

As to the house itself, James Wentworth Day told me a remarkable story of the haunting which, he claimed, caused one owner after another to sell up at any price and get out as quickly as possible. He genuinely felt there was a mælstrom of malice which still pervaded Edwin's Hall in the middle of the twentieth century. He had evidence of a table beautifully laid for dinner down to the last silver candlestick which was stripped completely in the seconds that the house-maid turned her back on it to draw the curtains. Everything on that table had been returned to its proper place in or on the sideboard, and all in utter silence. That is what caused the maid to leave and the owner to sell.

But there was more than that - there was the Evil Aura. In one room such an atmosphere was felt, like the humidity and stillness of a gathering thunderstorm, combined with the damp and dismal smell of the remains of the dead in a church vault. This, I was told, was the manifestation of the spirit of a nun who lived here in the Archbishop's time, murdered by a wandering sailor-turned-beggar for the sake of a few coins. Her spirit cannot rest. Even the builder called in to do some repair work thirty years ago said he definitely saw her face at the window, and that was in broad daylight. After that he made sure he finished every day long before it grew dark.

GREAT LEIGHS

Why do so many Essex inns have ghosts? I have been on the trail of just a few. If it is spirits of the spectral kind you are after, head for the St. Anne's Castle at Great Leighs on the Braintree road. This is one of the claimants to be the oldest licensed public house in the country which started as a hermitage where pilgrims on their way to St. Edmund's shrine could put up for the night. As you stand in its car park think of more modern times, say sixteen hundred-and-something, look around you for the large stone which once marked the grave of a witch, hanged at Chelmsford and buried at a crossroads on the Boreham side of the parish. Her bones were bulldozed up by the Americans constructing Boreham airfield in the last war, and now, some folks declare, her spirit haunts the bar-rooms. A brewer's delivery man swore he sensed 'something' in the cellar and would not go down there again for love or money; and last and least a teenage girl is reported to have fainted at the sight of a phantom in the fireplace just too fearful for her to describe.

Ghost hunters might like to try the Bell at Sible Hedingham. The landlady's sister came to stay, and in the night all the bed-clothes were suddenly whipped off her. The same thing happened to her daughter when she tried that room. They got in a medium who went into a trance and then declared that this room had been occupied at some time in its long history by a dark-haired woman who told her, in confidence of course, that she had been so happy at the Bell when alive that she wanted to stay there forever in spirit. Could you get a better advertisement?

The Angel, in Notley Road, Braintree has a wonderful history of haunting recorded over more than twenty years. A cheerful chappie, never seen, has switched on lights, opened doors, rearranged bottles and glasses. It might seem to disbelievers as very much like a case of 'Mr. Nobody' being responsible. But there is also a nasty sensation on the stairs, and disembodied voices, and phantom footsteps; though they are only heard when there is a change of landlord or layout. Obviously some of these ghosts are very conservative creatures.

St Anne's Castle, Great Leighs

14

BLACK NOTLEY

Such a family row blew up in 1589. Mary Bundocke was living in John Catterall's house in Black Notley - she might have been his servant, or his mistress, in those days many a servant girl was expected to be both. Her brother, Richard, did not like this state of affairs and remonstrated with her on several occasions, but she rounded on him - how she lived her life was her own affair.

He grew so angry and frustrated with her obstinacy in living with John Catterall that he went to see them on a cold, dark February evening - with an axe. He broke down their door and rushed at his sister as she sat there with John in the candlelight. He struck her four times with that axe and gave her what the court record calls, "four mortal wounds, two on the head and another on the back of her head an inch-and-a-half long and an inch deep into her brain, of which she instantly died." John Catterall was too surprised and then horrified by this dreadful attack to intervene and then Richard Bundocke was slashing at him. That same court record tells us: "The jurors say that Richard Bundocke, as above, broke into the house of the said John and assaulted him with an axe and gave him three mortal wounds, one on the right side of his head two inches long and half-an-inch deep, another of the same measurements on the left side of his head, a third with a knife, two inches long and into his brain, and, holding him, struck him in the throat and gave him a wound an inch long and two inches deep, whereof he instantly died."

Then Bundocke got his brother Robert to help him bury the two of them in their own backyard. There had been far too much noise for these dreadful deeds to go un-noticed. Neighbours sent for the village constable and he took the brothers into custody after disarming them. They languished in jail at Colchester for five months until they could be brought before the Assize Court at Chelmsford. The evidence was cut and dried; Robert Bundocke was found to be not guilty and was freed from custody, but Richard was found guilty, taken out of court and hanged there and then on the gallows.

BRENTWOOD

There's nothing new under the sun. You think the fun run is an invention of the younger generation? There was a man who did not just run, but danced, all the way through Essex, through Suffolk and Norfolk too; and that was as long ago as 1599. William Kemp was a comic actor in Shakespeare's company. He had the idea of making a little money by morris-dancing all the way from London to Norwich in nine days, with rest days and nights in between.

On the first day he not only danced all the way to Ilford, but carried on, in the moonlight, to Romford, with his two companions playing a drum and a whistle-pipe. There he rested for a couple of days, "...to give rest to well labour'd limbes" as he put it in his account of his amazing dancing marathon, which he called *Kemp's Nine Daies Wonder*. Then he goes on: " ...

and so merrily to Burnt-wood [*i.e.* Brentwood]. Yet, now I remember it well, I had no great cause for mirth, for at Romford townes end I strained my hip, and for a time indured exceeding paine; but being loath to trouble a Surgeon, I held on, finding remedy by labour that had hurt mee, for it came in a turne, and so in my daunce I turned it out of my service againe ... Having rested well at Burnt-wood, the moone shining clearly, and the weather being calme, in the evening I tript it to Ingerstone, stealing away from those number of people that followed mee; yet doe what I could, I had above fiftie in the company, some of London, the other of the country thereabouts, that would needs, when they heard my Taber, trudge after mee through thicke and thin.

"On Friday morning I set forward towardes Chelmsford, not having past two hundred, being the least company that I had in the day-time between London and that place. Onward I went thus easily followed, till I come to Witford-bridge, where a number of country people, and many Gentlemen and Gentlewomen were gathered to see me. Sir Thomas Mildmay, standing at his Parke pale, received gently a payre of garters of me; gloves, points and garters being my ordinary marchandize, that I put out to venture for performance of my merry voyage."

Let's leave him dancing still up the Braintree road, of which he says, "This foule way I could finde no ease in, thick woods being on eyther side the lane." You'll be glad to know he did make it all the way to Norwich.

Kemps nine daies vvonder,

Performed in a daunce from London to Norwich.

Containing the pleasure, paines and kinde entertainment of William Kemp betweene London and that Citty in his late Morrice.

Wherein is somewhat set downe worth note; to reprooue the slaunders spred of him: many things merry, nothing hurtfull.

Written by himselfe to satisfie his friends.

LONDON

Printed by E. A. for Nicholas Ling, and are to be solde at his shop at the west doore of Saint Paules Church. 1600.

William Kempe

16

FAULKBOURNE

Back in 1606 you had to go to the Quarter Sessions court to get permission to build a new house. That is what the Overseers of the parish of Faulkbourne did to help a poor lame woman, Susan Frost, and her two children. The Overseers had already approached the Lord of the Manor, owner of all the land around, and asked him if they might find a corner of his 'waste' - land not being cultivated - and build a cottage there. The Lord agreed, the cottage was built, but the Overseers had forgotten to get the permission of the Quarter Sessions. So they had to go before the court and beg that the cottage might be allowed to stand.

But the court had also received a letter from Maldon written by no less than the Bishop of London, the Suffragan Bishop of Colchester, Sir William Ayloff and other people of local standing. It said that they had been told by the Vicar of Faulkbourne that Susan Frost was 'a very incontinent woman having had sundry base-born children and not leaving her incontinent life' - even though she had been warned several times. Yet now, they heard, she was to be placed 'in a new erected house of purpose built for her in the King's highway very near the minister's house' and that, 'By her sole habitation she shall have fit opportunity to continue her bad course of life to the high displeasure of Almighty God.' In other words, as we might put it today, what was to stop turning this nice new house into a one-woman brothel? So the writers of the letter begged the court ' ... that the said house

may be removed and the woman punished for her incontinent life.

Hard words we might say, but how innocent was Susan Frost? She was involved in another matter at the same court when Miles Dawson, a Witham bricklayer was charged, on her oath, of 'Having carnal knowledge of her body whereby she thinketh that she is with child by him.' The inhabitants, led by the minister, did not want the child, when born, to be a charge on their parish, paid for out their rates, when Dawson should be made to pay the full cost of his sins.

Now, four hundred years later, unmarried mothers are still trying to get the fathers of their children to answer to their responsibilities.

St German, Faulkbourne

BRAINTREE

People think that life today becomes more violent. One reason may be that radio and television seek for endless sensation rather than news, in order to claim more listeners and viewers. There's not much doubt about it that local papers are the best reflection of life as it is lived in its fascinating variety in town and village. But let me offer a balance to the violence of present times by drawing your attention to an entry in the Essex Assize records for 1608.

Early on the day before Christmas Robert Adler, just ten years old, was already away from home, working hard, bound as an apprentice to John Nynnam in Braintree. How he offended his master we shall never know, but Nynnam decided to teach the little boy a lesson. With the help of Jeremy Eskland, working with him as a weaver, he tied Robert up, leaving him hanging from the loom's stout beam. Then he pulled down the boy's hose, his trousers, and began whipping him with a vicious whipcord, knotted at intervals along its length to make it that much more painful. Surely his screams must have been heard all down the Braintree road? But no-one made a move to stop him. Then Eskland weighed in. The boy was cut down and Eskland beat young Robert about the head with a cudgel and threw him down the stairs.

Poor Robert was left to crawl to his crude bed on the floor more dead than alive and later that same night, Christmas Eve, he died miserably.

Now the Constable for the town of Braintree was called, and the process of justice began. Henry Long, the Coroner, carried out his inquest and the blame for the boy's death was declared to be the result of that awful assault by those two wicked men. They were thrown into prison, to be tried at the next Quarter Sessions. They pleaded not guilty, after all, they were only beating a servant for misbehaviour! That did not convince jury who found both men guilty. The death sentence was inevitable. In no time at all they were taken from the courtroom, in the Sessions House, in Chelmsford, now known as the Shire Hall, and hanged on the gallows just off Rainsford Lane, where it meets Waterhouse Lane.

DUNTON WAYLETT

Many years ago on my wanderings through Essex I cycled down to Dunton Waylett, the 'town on the hill where the highways meet' and the old parish church, now a private house. I looked through the old parish records kept in the church chest and came across a page which caught my eye and fired my imagination. It was a real slice of village life, traced out by the Church Clerk with his quill pen, so faded now that I had to get out my magnifying glass to decipher it:

"May 2nd, 1612. Thomas Allan his confession and submission made before us whose names are underwritten:

"I, Thomas Allan, do here in the presence of God and this whole assembly freely and willingly acknowledge and confess against myself that I have here before in the great abuse of my tongue

18

spread abroad most uncharitably and slanderously these, or such like words, touching the dishonesty of Richard Stoward, servant and Anne Mason, the wife of William Mason, that they were seen naughty together in the abuse of their bodies under a shock of corn in harvest time, for which so uncharitable and slanderous words speaking I do first upon the great sorrow and grief of my heart crave pardon at the hand of Almighty God and do also entreat you Richard Stoward and Anne Mason to forgive me ... promising by the grace of God hereafter amendment both in the usage of my tongue and carriage of my whole life or else I will have this public act of mine to stand in record as witness against me."

Thomas had to stand in front of the whole congregation in church on a Sunday morning and make this apology - and all for saying that Richard Stoward was, as we might put it today, `having a little bit on the side.' This faded page had more impact on me than all my school history lessons rolled into one. Thomas's outburst can be understood when we read of him having `to appear and answer, touching the conveying away of Ellen Allan, his daughter, the mother of a base child born in the parish of Langdon Hills'. It seems that his girl, still very young, had given birth to this child away from home and parents, so off he went and brought her back - an act of love and desperation. This must have coloured his attitude to illicit love.

GREAT WALTHAM

Here is a story to while away a winter's night when the wind whines round the houses and the candle dances in the draught through the door. Since a Bishop of Gloucester vouched for its veracity we can surely believe that it must be true.

It happened three hundred years ago in the big house at Great Waltham called Langleys where Lady Everard then lived. Her brother, Sir Charles Lee, had a wife who was expecting a baby, but sadly at the birth the mother died and the child lived. Lady Everard offered to bring the baby up as her own and the little girl grew up as a happy and contented child in her aunt's tender care until the day when she came of age, and a marriage to Sir William Perkins was arranged. For some reason or other, perhaps Lady Everard could not afford the dowry demanded, the marriage never too place, much to the disappointment of the Lady and the fair Miss Lee.

Did this setback affect her mind? All we know is that in 1662 the poor girl woke up one night in her bedroom at Langleys with the distinct idea that there was a candle still burning in the room. She called for her maid who assured her that neither candle nor fire had been alight to cause the strange luminescence her mistress described. Comforted she fell asleep again, but at about two o'clock in the morning she was aroused by the appearance of a little old woman standing inside the bed curtains which were drawn all round, and bending closely over her. The old woman whispered hoarsely that her real mother was very happy in heaven and that at midday of that very morning she would be with her.

Very frightened by this apparition, Miss Lee took time to compose herself then she sent for her maid, who helped her to dress. She sat down and wrote a letter to her father and handed it into the care of Lady Everard, telling of the weird prophecy she had experienced. Her aunt sent straightaway for the doctor who could find nothing wrong with her in explanation of the strange story. Then the poor girl asked that the household's chaplain might say prayers with her. At the stroke of twelve she sat down in a chair, took two deep, sighing breaths - and died.

BILLERICAY

Tyrell is a good old Essex name. It goes all the way back to the men who came across the Channel with William the Conqueror in 1066. The last male in the main branch of the Essex family was Sir John Tyrell who died at Borcham House in 1877. A guide book of 1880 tells us that Heron Hall, in East Horndon was "...a fine mansion demolished in 1798 and formerly the residence of the Tyrell family." Going back even further it was in 1695 that John Tyrell of Billericay wrote down a story told by his great-grandfather Sir Henry Tyrell of Heron Hall, which he in turn was told by his grandfather. It goes like this:

Heron Hall

Merchants who traded with tribes in far-away Africa brought home a great serpent. When they anchored in the Thames that serpent escaped and swam ashore, creeping into the woods which lay between Heron Hall and the parish church of East Horndon. The rumour went round that it preyed on travellers along the high road, swallowing them whole and the whole neighbourhood became frightened. So their local lord, Sir James Tyrell, took on the mantle of St. George. Early one morning he donned his armour, sharpened his sword and had a large mirror hung round his neck. He took up his position beside the serpent's lair. Out popped the dreaded snake, saw his reflection in the mirror, and was stunned with surprise. Sir James was quick to wield his sword, slay the serpent and cut off its head which he carried home and presented to his wife whilst she still lay in her bed.

Sadly, he had worked himself up so much in killing the serpent that he had a heart attack and died. Some months later his son came upon the spot where the serpent's bones still lay. He kicked one of them away, crying, "This is the bone of the serpent which killed my father." The bone pierced his shoe, pricked his toe and gangrene set in which meant he had to have that leg cut off at the knee. Old Heron Hall, which once stood near where Heron House is now, had a window in which the portrait of this one-legged man was carried out in stained glass. You can still see a reminder of the Tyrells in the sign of the local hostelry, the Boar's Head, for that was the family crest.

WORMINGFORD

We see today how people, frustrated by what they feel is the ponderous plodding of the law, take justice into their own hands and attack those people in their community who they consider to be guilty of theft, assault and vandalism. That feeling has been about for a very long time, as witness this story.

In 1713 the village of Wormingford, northwest of Colchester, was buzzing with scandal and gossip. So many things were going wrong - children ill, animals dying, cream that would not churn, crops that failed. Somebody, they said, must be responsible for it all - a witch must have cast her evil spells. Who could that be? They settled on a little old lady who lived on her own after her husband had died, Elizabeth Micklefield. A gang of villagers, each with his own personal calamity to avenge, went along to her house and pulled her out of it across the green to the village pond.

It was commonly held in those days that you could tell a witch by the water test, so they threw Elizabeth into the pond. If she had floated it meant that even the basic element had rejected her body as too evil to be accepted by it. Then they would have put her to death by hanging or burning. But Elizabeth did not float, she sank, and drowned before their very eyes, without a hand to help her. Now they knew she was innocent, but dead. The village constable was called in. He took in charge all those involved - Mary, wife of John Smith, John Ambrose and his wife Mary, Mary the wife of John Lazell and labourer William Pudney.

They were all clapped in jail at Chelmsford until, nearly a year later, all enquiries had been made and they could be brought before the judge at the Assizes. None of them was found guilty except Mary Smith, who had given Elizabeth that last desperate push. She was taken out to the gibbet and hanged that same day. The others all went back to Wormingford at last and took up again the grinding daily task of getting enough to feed and clothe their families. No doubt they shook their heads at the injustice of it all, especially if, with the warmth of summer, and a good harvest in the offing, all those ailments of man and beast at Wormingford just seemed to fade away.

HIGH EASTER

Man is such a master of his environment that he now brings up natural gas from deep down under the North Sea. 250 years ago this phenomenon of gas creeping up to the surface in Essex was considered a manifestation of God's anger. It certainly was more than a nine days wonder when workmen began to dig out and shore up a well in High Easter in November, 1746.

What they came across was so extraordinary that it was fully recorded in 1805 in a book called *The Wonderful Museum and Gazette Extraordinary*. For the first twenty feet. "... the soil was a chalky clay, and they then came to a blackish earth, which lasted twenty-four

High Easter shop

feet more ... no water yet appeared. At thirty-eight feet they began to bore ... came to a sandy gravel so hard that the earth-bit would not penetrate, when they heard a noise, like water, and put some into the hole to soften the ground which immediately bubbled with a considerable noise, and continued till they dug down to the gravel, which was as hot as a horse-dung hill; they bored eleven feet more, when, a sulphurous smoke coming up the hole, they poured more water into it, and that bubbled as before and made a great noise, like a water-mill wheel.

"The master, finding himself faint, made the signal and was drawn up; then the servant, who did not stay to take the tools; his face and hands were almost black, and he was almost dead but he soon recovered in the open air. No water came into the well, but a strong wind blew up the hole which continued till next morning, when it burst up in so furious a torrent, that it threw up some of the sandy gravel and stones several feet above the mouth; and for a minute shook the farmhouse and the ground about it very much. After this, three cats being successively let down, one died; and lighted candles being no sooner put into the well, but they were extinguished."

They left that well for a fortnight, then ventured down again to retrieve their tools. A month later the farmer could still hear that rushing noise down in the well, but never a drop of water did they get. Today not even the oldest inhabitant can tell you where that well was.

BEAUMONT

If you like a love story, stop right here. In 1720 a baby girl was born to the wife of Robert Canham, a well-to-do farmer who lived in Beaumont Hall, in the tiny village of the same name, to the east of Tendring. They called her Kitty. She grew into a charming, attractive young lady who caught the eye and ensnared the heart of the Reverend Alexander Gough, Vicar of Thorpe-Le-Soken, the adjoining village. He proposed, she consented and her parents were delighted that she should make such a very good marriage.

But Thorpe-le-Soken was very little different from Beaumont. Kitty realised there was a big world out there, waiting to be explored with new excitements, new people round every corner. Disillusioned with life as vicar's wife, restless and seemingly unfulfilled, Kitty suddenly left home one day without a word to her husband or her parents, changed her name, and headed for London and the high life where all enquiries proved fruitless.

It was by chance that in the company of conspiring friends she met Lord Dalmeny, son of the Earl of Rosebery. He fell desperately and deeply in love with her and begged her to marry him. She could not tell him her guilty secret. She married him - and their honeymoon stretched on and on. For four years they wandered round Europe, lost to the world in love. Then, in 1752, at Verona, Kitty became ill and the doctors offered no hope of recovery. When she knew that death was inevitable Kitty called for paper and pen and scrawled a note which read, "I am

23

the wife of the Reverend Alexander Gough, Vicar of Thorpe-le-Soken in Essex. My maiden name was Catherine Canham. My last request is to be buried at Thorpe."

That was a request very difficult to grant, yet her second 'husband' Lord Dalmeny, in love and grief, carried out her wish to the letter. First he sent a special message across Europe to the Reverend Gough, informing him of the strange situation so that the burial could be arranged. Then, posing as a Mr. Williams, a Hamburg merchant, he chartered a special ship to bring back his sweetheart's body, embalmed, in a wooden chest. On arrival in England customs officers boarded the ship, looking for smuggled goods. They ordered the chest to be opened, saw the body, and asked for an explanation. The secret was out!

St Leonard, Beaumont-cum-Moze

HALSTEAD

Be 'upwardly mobile' today and you are rather disparagingly called a Yuppie, but three hundred years ago men were admired for their flair in speculation and in property dealing. Take John Morley, for example. He was born in 1656, the son of a Halstead butcher. He grew up to be apprenticed to his father in their shop where he became a master butcher in his own right after the death of his father. He would probably have continued butchering carcases and selling joints to the end of his life but for a chance remark from one of his customers, there in his shop, right by the church gate.

Sir Josiah Child, a governor of the East India Company had an estate near Halstead. Coming into the shop one day to buy his meat he said in the friendliest way that John Morley would be on to a good thing if he bought shares in the East India Company. Morley, certain of his smaller but sure butcher's profits said that he would rather buy fat sheep. The good Sir Josiah prevailed upon him to risk a hundred pounds in the venture. The shares rose so much in value that he reaped a hundred per cent profit, took it and left the original sum still invested. He told his wife that, to please her he would not risk those profits again but would buy property with them.

That property, when sold, made him even richer and his further property dealings made butchery almost a sideline. But he still kept his old, open ways with rich and poor and his strength of character attracted new friends - landowners, politicians, poets, whom he entertained at his new home Blue Bridge House. They included the poets Matthew Prior, his particular friend, and Alexander Pope. He had been helped into this exciting new world by Robert Harley, Earl of Oxford, in return for Morley's arranging the very profitable marriage of the Earl's son to the heiress of the Duke of Newcastle in 1713.

To prove to himself and to his new friends that he had not forgotten his old way of life he went to Halstead market once a year and in a kind of ceremony killed and cut up a pig in full view of old friends, new friends and former customers, and what a fuss they made of him.

CANVEY ISLAND

Where would we be without our up-to-the moment news reports in papers and on television and radio? In 1953 we had instant news of the terrible flooding of Canvey Island. Two hundred years before there had been a very high tide which sent rumours of damage and destruction far inland. Four days after that tide the *Chelmsford Chronicle*, the county newspaper, published the facts:

The following letter having been received from a gentleman possessed of considerable property on Canvey Island, who, of course, must be well acquainted with the damage sustained, we are happy in presenting it to our readers:

"It having been asserted in the London papers, that this island had suffered irreparable damage by the late high tides, and that there were three immense breaches in the sea walls; I beg leave through the channel of your paper to contradict those reports; as they must have given much uneasiness to people who have property on the island. In fact there has been very little damage done to Canvey Island, everything considered; there was a small breach made near the sluice which was immediately stopped up; and this was the only breach made in the walls; it is true the water topped the walls, spread over a great part of the island, and, by filling the streets has, I fear, spoiled the fresh water for the summer, which must be a great inconvenience for the inhabitants. As to loss of stock, I can assure you there was only two sheep lost on the whole island; I am of opinion that the land has

Crossing from Canvey to Benfleet, 1910

received but little injury, as our fields of wheat are as fine and green as any in Essex; and the sea water is now quite gone off except in the very lowest places. The account in the London papers must have been inserted by some evil-minded person with the most illiberal intention."

At the same time John Harriott was writing of Rushley Island, which he had embanked, "I can with pleasure inform you, that my island was overflowed (merely from the excess of the tide) but there was no breach, and when the tide fell I was surprised to find the island left brim full, like a bowl-dish, the outside of my walls did not receive a guinea damage. I was then obliged to cut through the walls in several places, to let out the water." So I suppose we could say that on this occasion the rumours were just a storm in teacup.

26

BILLERICAY

Thomas Wood was a miller so strong that he could carry two sacks of flour at a time. Born in 1719 in Great Burstead he grew up to be the miller at Billericay Mills - a pair of windmills either side of the road from Billericay to South Green and Great Burstead, known locally as the Bell Hill Mills. He was a classic example of the subject of an old song, Michael Finnigan who "grew fat and then grew thin again..." He was brought up by indulgent parents to enjoy his food, and plenty of it, fat meat three times a day, with bread, butter, cheese and plenty of ale to wash it down. By 1764 when he was 45 he was subject to all kinds of illness, including gout, rheumatism, flatulence, and breathlessness and he had become dangerously obese.

The Rector of Nevendon, who knew him well, seeing his deterioration, suggested he should read the *Life of Cornaro*, which included good advice on the sense of a sober and moderate diet. He did, and it convinced him that overeating and drinking were the root causes of his problems. He became a teetotaller, gave up eating meat, began using dumb-bells for exercise and took a cold bath twice a week. He must have lost at least eleven stone, but that could not be established because he was too superstitious to sit on a weighing machine. From 1767 he ate no food other than a kind of dumpling made each day from a pound of flour boiled in one and a half pints of milk. When he had to spend the day at Romford market he took the ingredients with him and had them boiled up at the inn. His regimen gave him fifteen more years of life; he was 63 when he died.

His case was published in Sir George Baker's *Medical Transactions*, where it is said, "... he is metamorphosed from a monster to a person of moderate size, from the condition of an unhealthy decrepit old man, to perfect health, and to the vigour and activity of youth..." But the name he had gained in his corpulent days still stuck; behind his back he was called the Ghastly Miller, though more sympathetic folk, witnessing his dramatic reduction in size and diet called him the Abstemious Miller.

The *Mayflower* windmill, Billericay, which collapsed 1928

LATCHINGDON

Today we take a cup of tea for granted; so easy to get from the corner shop or the supermarket, in Chinese-looking tins or in teabags in a big packet. We forget that it comes from the other side of the world. It was not until around 1710 that Thomas Garraway, proprietor of a coffee-house in London, got hold of a chest or two of tea to introduce to his customers as the latest fashion. He could never have imagined the hold the new beverage would establish in Britain and wherever Britons wandered in the service of the Empire.

It was not until late in the eighteenth century that Essex villagers first saw and tasted this drink which had caught the fancy of London gentry. All Latchingdon was talking about it around 1775 when John Laver, a local man of some wealth, came back from London one day carrying a surprise present for his wife. It was a pound of the new 'tea' for which he had paid more than a guinea. Out of his carriage he also brought a complete tea-making set which included a tea caddy in which to keep the prized leaves, a tea-kettle with a handle specially jointed to fall over sideways, just liked they used in China, a teapot and, of course, the necessary cups and saucers.

How the servants gaped and told all their friends, and the village as a whole all about it. When Mr. Laver's groom's wife was brought to bed of a child Mrs. Laver, kindly employer, went to her house to show her concern and to offer help. In her pleasure at a safe and healthy birth she offered all the assembled ladies a cup of tea - what excitement. The groom was sent to fill the tea-kettle from the waterbutt, the only source of drinking water. He was gone so long that Mrs. Laver had to send someone after him. The reason for his delay was that he had never seen such a strange vessel as that Chinese tea-kettle before. He did not know that the kettle lid came off, so was patiently trying to fill it by pouring water down its spout with the aid of a jug.

CHIGWELL

Two hundred years ago the manufacturers of patent medicines made the most amazing claims for their products, and went to great lengths to give realism to their advertisements. For example, in the *Chelmsford Chronicle* of 25th April, 1777, right in the middle of a news column, between the story of a reprieve given by the King to a prisoner in Ipswich gaol, and the account of two French ships in a chase after their British counterparts, there is a letter, cunningly inserted.

It purports to come from a Mr. George Scott of Woolston Hall, Chigwell, and is addressed to a Mr. Francis Newbery, who happens to be the manufacturer of Dr. James Analeptic pills. It runs thus:

"As I have been full six months cured by Dr. James's Analeptic pills of an universal rheumatism, with which I had been five years, I may say, tormented, I think gratitude calls on me to let you know it; and from the common dictates of humanity, to give you leave to make what use you please of this letter. It may be

A cure-all of the 1850s

proper here to mention, that the very first dose of two pills had a most astonishing effect, and was accordingly much taken notice of by a near relation I was then with at Oxford, who had seen the state I had then been in. I have since, at times, tho' not often, taken one or two pills to prevent a relapse. I thought it a duty incumbent on me last Sunday to return public thanks for this very extraordinary cure ... your very humble servant, George Scott."

Then, almost by the way, we read that Dr. James's Analeptic pills are sold by B. C. Frost and S. Gray at Chelmsford, by W. Keymer at Colchester, by J. Smitheman at Braintree and J. Giffin at Brentwood. What a masterpiece of copywriting. I would hazard the guess that George Scott, who really did live in Woolston Hall and was a qualified lawyer, had shares in the business. After an advertisement like that they should have made a nice profit. And what do you think `analeptic' means? - Nothing more than `comforting'.

GREAT STAMBRIDGE

John Harriott was an Essex man, born in Great Stambridge in 1745. He had a great life of travel and adventure in England and America before he died in 1817. From travelling the world as a midshipman in the Royal Navy he became a merchant seaman, a member of an American Indian tribe and then a soldier in the East India Company until injury forced him to retire to Essex, around 1780.

He bought Rushley Island, between Great Wakering and Foulness for £40. Within ten years his house and barns were all burnt down. He rebuilt them, and in less than a year a great tide overwhelmed his island - house, crops, barns and animals - he was bankrupt. Off he went to America to make his fortune all over again. In five years he was back in Essex, still bubbling with life and optimism.

One of his schemes, to combat theft from ships in the Thames led directly to the establishment of the Essex River Police, but everybody seems to have forgotten the most unusual invention for which he was awarded a prize by the Society for the Encouragement of Arts, Manufactures and Commerce in 1789. It was a road harrow - the world's first road repair machine. It happened because John Harriott had been appointed Surveyor of Highways for his parish of Great Stambridge in 1786. Riding up and down its roads he was appalled at their condition. Heavy wagons drawn by up to eight horses at a time had caused such ruts that other traffic got stuck in the sticky Essex clay. Stones put back by the road-man were displaced by the next leviathan.

Harriott himself tells us: "I therefore contrived the road harrow, by the help of which I have, at a very trifling expense to the Parish, kept the roads in extraordinary good condition. A man, a boy and two horses will do three miles in length in one day, completely harrowing down the quarters and drawing the stones together, which, by means of the mould boards are dropped into the rut far better than a man can stub them in." His harrow, all of wood, looked much like a front-to-back snowplough, with fearsome iron spikes which tore at the mounds between the ruts. Behind them two boards turned all the loosened stones back into the ruts and tamped it all down.

That Society was so impressed with Harriott's harrow that he was awarded a prize of ten guineas, and that was when ten guineas was worth ten guineas.

GOSFIELD

Gosfield is a pleasant village north of Braintree, with old houses harmoniously bordering the village street. But some of the half-timbered cottages look rather older than they are. They were erected to the order of Samuel Courtauld around 1860 when he was the lord of the manor, living at Gosfield Hall. He also provided the villagers with their hall. He was following in the footsteps of an earlier benefactor a century beforehand.

In the eighteenth century there was no local work for cottagers but on the land; wages were at subsistence level and bad weather sometimes meant no pay at all. One man who saw this was the lord of the manor, George Nugent-Temple-Grenville, made 1st Marquis of Buckingham in 1784. He had married the daughter of Lord Nugent and they came to live here in Gosfield. They took their position in the village very seriously and were anxious to do all they could to better the conditions for tenants and villagers alike.

In 1790 they saw an opportunity to improve their circumstances by encouraging the use of straw, a by-product of agriculture, to make straw-plaiting on a cottage industry basis. The straw cost nothing, farmers had an abundance of it, and when it was flattened and split by ingenious hand tools made at home it could be plaited into lengths which were then used to make all kinds of useful and decorative articles, with emphasis on straw hats which then were all the rage and gave the best returns.

The villagers were ready to have a go, but, of course, their first efforts were amateurish and folk were unwilling to buy. Lady Buckingham soon altered that; she bought a hat, put a bright ribbon on it and wore it conspicuously all round the village. She was the fashion setter for the area and all the farmers' wives soon followed. Then her husband the Marquis wore one to church one day and rested it on his pew in full view of the congregation - local gentry, farmers and traders followed suit. The straw-plaiters, mostly women and children, quickly improved with practice under the eyes of an expert brought from Dunstable by the Marquis. You can judge their success from the report in 1806 that Gosfield, with just 453 inhabitants, earned £1,700 in one year from their straw plaiting. That was a fortune indeed.

Gosfield Hall, 1831

EAST HANNINGFIELD

In the days when even the smallest village had to be self-sufficient in its water supply there must have been tremendous satisfaction in digging for water and finding it. In 1790 the good folk of East Hanningfield did not have a single decent, dependable well to keep them supplied on a daily basis through summer and winter alike. The parson honoured all his obligations to his parishioners, he saw the need and determined to fulfil it. He set workmen digging right there in his parsonage yard. It turned out to be such a difficult and lengthy undertaking that it was reported in the national press. Here is what a contributor to the *Gentleman's Magazine* of 8th July, 1791, wrote:

"Unacquainted as I am with the measurement of the deepest wells in this kingdom, I conjecture that the one at length fortunately completed by the Reverend Mr. Nottidge of East Hanningfield parsonage, near Chelmsford to be sufficiently extraordinary to merit your notice. It was begun on June 21st, 1790, and water, when the workmen from such tedious labour, were at the moment of despair, was found May 7th, 1791. Thirty-nine thousand five hundred bricks were used, without cement, in lining this well, the soil of which, for the first thirty feet was a fine, light-brown, imperfect marl; though fossilists may ingeniously choose to discriminate the different strata, yet, except from shades of a deeper colour and firmer texture, occasionally, but slightly, mixed with a little sand and a few shells, the same soil, to a common eye, without material variation, continued to 450 feet, where it was consolidated into so rocky a substance as to require being broken through with a mattock. A bore then, of 3 inches in diameter and 15 feet in length was tried, which soon, through a soft soil, slipped from the workman's hands and fell up to the handle. Water instantly appeared and rose within the first hour 150 feet, and after a very gradual rise, now stands at 347 feet, extremely soft and well-flavoured ..."

It had taken eleven months of endless digging and clambering up and down the ever-extending ladders. The parson paid for it all, for the benefit of all the villagers, irrespective of their religious beliefs, "For whose use it is always open," he declared - truly a good man.

PURFLEET

The Purfleet to Dartford tunnel is a modern marvel, allowing road traffic to sweep speedily around the M25. It certainly is a miracle of technical know-how, but few people realise that this tunnel had its origin in the mind of a forgotten man as far back as 1798.

He was Ralph Dodd, civil engineer, who went down to the south bank of the Thames to make a survey, `... as might enable him to bring the subject before the public...' He reckoned that a tunnel could be excavated and totally completed, including the installation of a steam-engine to pump out drainage water, for a total of £15,995. At a public meeting in 1798 he claimed that the cost could be reduced by £3,141 by the sale of the excavated chalk and flint.

By the following February shares to a total of £30,000 had been taken up and everything looked rosy for this daring undertaking. A special Act of Parliament was passed in 1799 and work began on the initial borings. A snag cropped up; they had only got down forty-two feet when water poured into the bore more quickly than their primitive horse-driven pump could extract it. That steam engine Dodd had mentioned was now urgently required. They just had to buy it, and blow the expense; but the shareholders' money was fast disappearing. The engineers needed to get down one hundred and forty-five feet to pass safely under the Thames, but there was another setback. The steam pump had been installed by May, 1802, but in the following October a disastrous fire destroyed the engine house and the shoring in the shaft.

This was the knock-out blow. Restoration was beyond the company's resources. It limped on with a token effort at forwarding the boring, but in May, 1810, the last company meeting was adjourned and no date was set for another. In 1935 Essex and Kent County Councils resurrected the idea as a solution to the problem of increasing through traffic in the London area - but the Ministry of Transport rejected it 'on grounds of national economy'. So we waited until 18th November, 1963, to make that simple journey from Essex to Kent.

CHIPPING ONGAR

"Twinkle, twinkle little star,
    How I wonder what you are ..."

We all know that dear old nursery rhyme; but did you know that it is not as old as all that; that it was written in Essex; that the poet was a young girl called Jane Taylor? The Taylors, parents and children, were a talented bunch. Father Isaac was a minister in the Congregational church and a very clever engraver, illustrating editions of the Bible, Shakespeare, Goldsmith and other well-known authors. Mother Ann, was the authoress of books on house-wifery. Among their children were Ann, born in 1782, Jane, born in 1783 and Isaac, born in 1787. In service of the church they moved from Lavenham to Colchester in 1796, then on to Ongar in 1811, living first at Castle House and then, from 1814, at Peaked Farm.

It was while they were living in Colchester, in 1806, that Jane and Ann published their second book of poems, called *Rhymes for the Nursery*. In it was Jane's world-famous poem, "Twinkle, twinkle little star." That one poem caught the public imagination wherever English was spoken. It was learned willingly by infants at the their mothers' knees. Most of us never got past the first verse. Did you know that there are five verses? The last goes like this:

"As your bright and tiny spark
Lights the traveller in the dark,
Though I know not what you are,
Twinkle, twinkle, little star."

Jane died in 1824 and was buried in the Congregational churchyard in Ongar.

View near the Royal Forest Hotel, Epping Forest, 1911

EPPING FOREST

The Forest is a lovely place for a day out with a picnic lunch; parking the car and walking miles in woodland greenery right on London's doorstep. While you are walking think of the days, two hundred years ago when highwaymen like Dick Turpin made the forest frightening. I will reassure you with a story which shows violence was averted by ignorance and superstition.

The stage coach had set out from the Bull Inn, Bishopsgate, heading for Cambridge through Epping Forest which a poet of the day described as:

A dreary landscape, bushy and forlorn,

Where rogues start up like mushrooms in a morn;

The forest was indeed notorious for the bands of armed criminals, many of them soldiers discharged after the Napoleonic Wars, who lived in rough camps in the trees and preyed on travellers up the old Roman road.

On this stage coach the conversation had turned to the possibility of just such an attack. The passengers joked about what they would do - hiding their true fear. At that moment a great shout of "Stand and deliver!' sent a shiver down every backbone. Bandits were seen, half-hidden in the greenery while their leader and his lieutenant clambered up to the coach door and demanded gold from everyone - only gold would do. The passengers could do nothing but turn out their pockets. One man, a humble journalist, had no gold. He offered his silver coins but this so enraged the bandit leader that the frightened man, scrabbling in his satchel for money, spilled the contents on to the floor of the coach.

The bandit looked down - saw all the journalist's sheets of paper covered in shorthand (introduced by Samuel Taylor in 1786) and in his brute ignorance took them for some secret incantation. "Damnation! What's this? - I'm off!" He jumped down and fled with his men into the forest. Once clear of the trees and out in the sunshine that journalist looked very smug - he was the only passenger who had not been robbed.

BARKING

Barking has developed through the centuries from a fishing port to a commercial and industrial centre, with offices and factories crowding down to the banks of Barking Creek where the river Roding joins the Thames. It is hard to believe that this place was once a port of great significance. From its quay for years there sailed the greatest fishing fleet the world has ever seen. In 1814 when the quay was rebuilt there were 70 ships tying up there, each of between 40 and 53 tons. By 1833 there were 133 such vessels sailing out of the creek into the North Sea.

Owner of the largest number was Samuel Hewett, who gained fame and fortune for his family firm - the Short Blue Fleet - by introducing the very first,

Barking Town Quay, 1900

primitive refrigeration of the catch from fishing grounds to port. He arranged for the marshes around the town to be flooded as winter approached. The ice produced by the cold weather was broken up by a gang of labourers and carried into an icehouse, specially dug deep into the earth where it would stay frozen for months.

On every fishing trip one fast-sailing cutter accompanied the fleet, with ice in its hold. It collected all the fish as they were caught by the smacks and, while those smacks stayed out on their fishing stations, the loaded ice-ship put on all sail for Barking and so on to London up the Thames and that lucrative market. The late Sir William Addison explained the developing system: "The Short Blue Fleet was commanded by a senior skipper, known as 'The Admiral', who flew a special flag and by signal code gave orders for the lowering and pulling in of the nets. This system necessitated the redesigning of smacks, which could now be larger, since speed for bringing in the fish was no longer the main consideration. Each of these new smacks went out with rations for six weeks, although fresh supplies to supplement the rations were brought on each trip by the carrier ... "

Many of the crew of the fishing fleet were recruited from local orphanages. Their lodging ashore between trips and their general welfare were put in the hands of Samuel Hewett's wife who was the 'Admiral' of a large group of women helpers. The high point of the Short Blue Fleet was in 1850 when no less than 225 smacks made a grand sight as they sailed down the Thames to their fishing grounds.

BRAINTREE

The factory workers thought so much of their boss that they clubbed together to give him a special dinner and an illuminated address of praise. It happened to a very well-known employer in 1846 That man was Samuel Courtauld. When most of his family had gone to America to make their fortune, he stayed on in Braintree, running a silk-weaving factory in Panfield Lane. He expanded it in 1817, fell out with his partner and moved on to Bocking where there was a watermill to provide all his power. Here he introduced the manufacture of crêpe, much in demand then for funeral and mourning dress. By 1822 Samuel was able to say with pride that he was now earning a thousand pounds a year.

With capital behind him Samuel could buy the Town Mill in Halstead in 1825 and convert it to the making of crêpe on contract. Now he had three factories and his work force was doubled - good news for the many people in rural Essex thrown out of work by the agricultural depression. He achieved a wonderful reputation; C. Fell Smith said in the *Essex Review*: "Both Mr. and Mrs. Courtauld looked personally after the welfare of their workpeople, and were untiring in their efforts for the education, amusement, sustenance, and good housing of every man, woman or child whom they employed."

Houses with the Courtauld monogram on their gables in Bocking and Halstead are still sheltering happy families. Samuel Courtauld once said, "When I die, I should like to have written on my tomb, `He built good cottages.'" He certainly did! No wonder then that, in 1846, sixteen hundred workers at the three mills got together to present him with a silver medallion and an illuminated address at a dinner they arranged in a huge marquee in a field right next to the Courtauld family home at High Garrett in Bocking Street.

The medal carried on one side the arms of the Weavers' Company and was inscribed `Honour to who honour is due"

and, `Blessed is he that considereth the poor' and on the other side it says, `Long live the Company' and, `By winders aid our wealth is made.' All around the edge the message runs: `Dinner given to Samuel Courtauld ... by 1,600 of their people, June 26, 1846.' It was estimated that five thousand people in a four-abreast crocodile a mile long filed into that field to honour their employer and benefactor. What a sight! What a memory!

Braintree Market, 1826

RETTENDON

Bennywith the boxer fought in the days when the ring was just a patch of grass roped off in the meadow, gloves were unheard of, and, if you rested at all between rounds, you sat on your second's knee. He was known as the Essex Champion and a tough old bruiser he was. But he met his match in a field near Rettendon Common, where the football played today is an altogether gentler sport. Banned though such fights were, this match between the Essex Champion and Joshua Hudson, 'a first-rate pugilist, who beat Scroggins', was advertised widely enough to attract at least 7,000 spectators. The purse was no less than thirty guineas [£31.50], a very large sum when the fight took place, on 4th April, 1820.

The *Chelmsford Chronicle* then takes up the story: "The arena was a 24-feet roped ring, in which Hudson threw up his hat, at one o'clock precisely, and was shortly followed by Bennywith, who repeated the same token of defiance. Hudson was seconded by Tom Owen and Purcell and Bennywith by his brother and cousin.

The first round was well contested and Hudson kept his distance and avoided some slashing hits. In a rally, some blows were exchanged to the advantage of Hudson, but he was floored by a right hand teaser.

2. Hudson had found out the vulnerable points of his antagonist, and he unmuzzled at him and turned to gallantly. The Essex man threw away many blows, which were prevented telling by Hudson going manfully up to his adversary's head, and keeping at in-fighting. Bennywith was skilfully dropped by a flush facer.

3. Hudson led again, and exchequered his head by straight hitting until he stupefied him. Bennywith, however, hit away at random, and although floored again, some of his blows told. But it was Fenchurch-street to a fig.

4. This was the last round. Bennywith made his last effort, but he was met going in with such force, that he yielded without knowing of it. He was knocked down, and could not be made sensible to come to time, and Hudson won the stake."

The fight only lasted eight and a half minutes - a very short fight for those days, but the damage done to both men's brains lasted throughout their lives.

BRENTWOOD

Brentwood was quite a quiet place back in 1824. There was no railway then and the car had not been invented. The only litter in the streets was horse-droppings, and that was taken away soon enough for the townsfolks' vegetable patches. So, when the peace was disturbed it was all the more of a shock and the riot was more than a nine days' wonder.

It all happened because of a government regulation which said that standard-sized pewter pots must be introduced by all publicans in place of the old earthenware mugs which had for so long been in common use. This meant quite an expense for the publicans and the alehouse keepers, so they put it off as long as they could. A couple of Brentwood fellows read this regulation and saw that they could claim a reward for reporting to the authorities any public house or tavern where earthenware pots were still in use. Round the town they went and had nine landlords fined. They were going to collect their `earnings' from the court office when they were set upon by a mob of publicans and `regulars' who were mad at these `traitors'. They grabbed the two informers and dragged them through what the newspaper of the day called "a filthy place in the White Hart Inn yard". It was in fact the `bumby', or primitive public toilet, and the two men were covered in excrement, becoming as the paper puts it, "truly objects of commiseration."

The magistrate was in the White Hart at that very moment. He came out and read the Riot Act in very loud voice, got the informers under the guard of four constables and sent them to the Fleece Inn at Brook Street. But the rioters did not disperse, they followed the constables, recaptured the wretched informers and dragged them through the horse trough outside the Fleece after pelting them with cow-dung, rotten eggs and stones. But those rioters did not have the last laugh, more constables appeared and the twelve ringleaders of the riot were taken in charge. They were all sent to the Quarter Sessions court in Chelmsford where they were severely warned about their future conduct and given a month's hard labour while they cooled off.

GREENSTED GREEN

In 1834 practically the only work a man could get in the little Dorset village of Tolpuddle was on the land and that was badly paid. The imports of cereals and other foods from the Empire was cutting into farmers' profits and they, in turn, squeezed their labourers, reducing their wages. Grinding poverty bred desperate revolt, started by six labourers who formed a trade union and tried to start a strike. The laws of the day were evoked, the labourers were accused of fomenting unrest and, after a travesty of trial they were sentenced to transportation to an Australian penal colony for seven years. All England rose in protest; and within two years a full pardon was granted to all six men. They came home independently and all were back in England by 1839. The British public contributed to a fund to settle them on their own farms.

That was how three of them came to Essex, to New House Farm, based on Tudor Cottage and two others, Thomas and John Standfield were found a farm at High Laver. There is now a plaque on the wall of Tudor Cottage, Greensted Green which reads:

"On their return from transportation the Tolpuddle Martyrs, George Loveless, James Loveless and James Brine lived here from 1838 to 1844." From this very house James Brine walked down to the church to marry Thomas Standfield's daughter in 1839. Then things went wrong again, the Martyrs started a local branch of the Chartist Association, fighting for the extension of political power to the working classes. So many people flocked to their meetings that Tudor House could not fit them all in, they had to adjourn to one of the fields. The only time they could have such meetings was on a Sunday morning. The Vicar did not like that. It considerably reduced his congregation. The farmers did not like it either - they took it as a personal threat, and since they were backed by the local magistrates the Martyrs experienced the greatest hostility from everyone who did not wish to see the *status quo* upset.

Since the lease of the farm was for seven years only, the Martyrs decided to leave of their own accord and look for a freer environment. They found it in Ontario.

Tudor Cottage, Greensted, showing the plaque by the downstairs window

LITTLE BADDOW

What a set-out there was in the Rodney, down the hill at Little Baddow, on 20th December, 1838, when one drink led to another. It started with Jonathan Perkins and his wife having a quiet drink in the tap-room of the old Rodney (not so far down the hill as the present Rodney) when in came Joseph Lucking, his two sons Joseph and William and a bunch of friends, all noisy and excited. The Perkins raised their eyebrows at each other and tactfully retired to the room beyond. It was not long before William Lucking staggered in to enjoy a little teasing. He bent over Mrs. Perkins and asked for a drink of her beer. She indignantly refused him and what did he do but tread heavily and purposefully on her toes. Up jumped Mr. Perkins and told young Lucking off - in came Lucking senior and knocked Perkins back over his stool. When the poor man got to his feet Lucking grabbed him while his son beat him about the head and body. The Constable was called, the Luckings were arrested and spent a very unpleasant Christmas awaiting their trial on 11th January, 1839.

Then they told their side of the story, with two witnesses to support them, who said that old Lucking went to fetch his son out of the room when Mrs. Perkins struck him in the face, turned the others out of the room and pushed her husband off his stool. After this exhibition of her prowess, they said, Mrs. Perkins tucked up her sleeves and said she would fight any man in the tap-room. Both of them were positive that Mrs. Perkins struck the first blow. What a sorry story for the magistrates to sort out. They went into a huddle and decided that William Lucking's toe-treading had been clearly proved, so they inflicted a fine of 2s.6d. [12½p] on him and all the others, Perkins and Luckings, were bound over to keep the peace. One of the magistrates advised Perkins in future to send to the pub for his beer "and drink it by his cottage fire-side." For two families in Little Baddow Christmas that year was best forgotten.

It was a cold, dark night in February, 1842, when Mary Pullen, in her eighties, and her daughter Mary Nunn locked up the Old Rodney, and got themselves ready for bed. Both had lost their husbands, so there was not a man in the house. Yet there had never been any further trouble in the pub; all the customers were local men and their wives who were very protective of their dear old landlady.

Soon the two ladies were upstairs, snug in bed and fast asleep. They were woken all of a sudden by such a noise. In the darkness three men burst into their bedroom and by the light of a lantern they were waving about the frightened women saw they had bludgeons raised above their heads as they shouted, "It's money we want and it's money we'll have!" Immediately the ladies gave them all they had in the bedroom - 3s. 10d. - and told them there was more cash in the bar. The men went down there. There was no point in screaming for help, the place was too far away from the nearest house for them to be heard, and the men would not let them scream again. After an hour spent in ransacking the bar for bottles of spirits,

Old Rodney House

Old Rodney House

cash, and even packets of biscuits the thieves went back upstairs, forced the terrified ladies to shake hands with them and set off up the hill for Danbury.

It was a long time before the ladies could summon up the courage to creep downstairs and find they were safe, and on their own. Mary Nunn dashed round to neighbour Saward and he ran for the Little Baddow constable, Mr. Tucker. It was daylight as he looked round the Rodney, heard that biscuits had been taken, went out on to the road and spotted bits of broken biscuit leading up to Danbury. There he asked around and found someone who had seen, early that morning, three men carrying bottles, heading down the road to Maldon. Down that way P.C. Tucker ran,

asking travellers on the way if they had seen these men. So he came at last to the White Hart at Hazeleigh and there were two of the men, sitting at a table with their heads down on their arms, in drunken slumber. He delved into their pockets, found crumbs of some of those same biscuits and clapped them in handcuffs before they were properly awake.

There was no point in taking them back to Little Baddow, they were caught red-handed, as guilty as could be, so P.C. Tucker roused them and set out with them for Chelmsford and the prison up on Springfield hill. It was only fourteen years old then, quite a wonder of the age, with treadmills to keep the convicts employed and a great porch on top of which

42

hangings were carried out in full view of a gaping crowd.

These two ruffians, suffering the most appalling hangover and feeling very tired after their night's activity, shuffled back along the road to Chelmsford, urged on by the policeman and the threat of his staff, a good deal longer than today's truncheon. They had passed Woodham Walter with Danbury in sight when the wretches revolted. Each with his free arm hustled and bustled P.C. Tucker off the road and into a field. All three fell over and in the hurly-burly they wrenched the policeman's staff away from him, beating him with it and yelling, "Give us yer keys, you b----r or we'll kill you!" P.C. Tucker was able to call out loudly, "Help! Murder!' before they pressed him down and knelt on his chest and legs. It was the purest luck that someone heard that cry. Philip Tiffin and his mate were returning from Maldon on a big brewery wagon drawn by a team of horses, having made a delivery for Wells & Perry, the Chelmsford brewers. They had stopped to pass the time of day with a friend when, from high up on the wagon, Philip heard that cry and saw the fighting in the field.

With great presence of mind he leapt down from the wagon, dashed into the field, grabbed the policeman's staff from the villains and used it to restore law and order. The thieves were securely bound, put on the wagon and taken into Chelmsford where, at the police station, the Police Superintendent took away their shoes and compared them with the footprints made in the garden at the Old Rodney: they matched. At the Assizes the thieves were sentenced to be transported for life to the new colony in Australia, and Philip Tiffin was granted £5 for his bravery in assisting the policeman. That policeman had to be satisfied with a pat on the back for a job well done.

Oxney Green, 1906

WRITTLE

Not long ago Writtle was just a small village, worth a summer evening walk from Chelmsford to watch cricket on the green, to listen to the bellringers at practice and to pop in for a pint at the Cock and Bell. It surely could not have been the place where the hoi polloi flocked in noisy hullabaloo to see the races and have a flutter on their favourite horses? But it was, although I must admit it was a hundred and fifty years ago.

The racecourse was laid out on the Oxney Green side of Writtle. The local paper of 1846 reported: "Altogether there were far greater numbers than we have seen at Galleywood of late years; and probably there were little short of 10,000 people present. The whole of Oxney Green appeared alive with people, the course, which was in excellent order considering the season, being from the distance to the winning post, lined with carriages and other vehicles in some places two or three deep, and on the opposite side in the meadow engaged for the use of the stewards and their friends, wagons and other vehicles and a low scaffolding formed a continuous stand the whole length was densely filled."

There were booths set up to provide all kinds of refreshment and, "a set of excellent musicians; forming part of the Queen's private band, delighted the company with popular airs throughout the day. The great landowner of the area was Lord Petre and much of the success of Writtle Races was due to his patronage. Where he went with Lady Petre the socialites of the day followed, to see and to be seen. After some great racing, concluding with the Handicap Stakes, the stewards and their friends joined the Petres and their families and friends at *déjeuner* in a marquee where toasts were drunk, including the health of the noble Lord and his family. In reply Lord Petre denied reports by his political enemies that he had a `sinister motive' in supporting Writtle Races. He assured the company that he had "... no motive but that of contributing to the amusement of the neighbourhood, and especially of my own."

A jolly day ended with a vigorous dance in the marquee, "and the day closed as it had passed, with good order and delight."

BRADFIELD

The Smiths are a very big family! There is a very large number of them in Essex, and so there should be, for this is a county famous for its blacksmiths; very important men in the village when horses were the only form of transport as they `serviced' them with horseshoes just as often as we take our cars in for servicing today. What is more, every item of iron used in house-building, from the humble nail upwards, was made in the village forge.

No wonder then that a blacksmith's wedding brought other smiths and their families from miles around to enjoy the festivities. One custom they practised in the days of Good Queen Bess was called `Firing the anvil'. They brought their small anvils on their carts with them and ranged them round the village green. Each smith had bored a hole in his anvil in which he tamped down some gunpowder, plugged it and then fitted it with a short fuse. As the marriage was publicly blessed they lit their fuses and the series of extremely loud bangs that followed sounded like a rather ragged military salute.

The practice of this Essex custom was finally abandoned around 1850 because of a very unfortunate accident. John Scrivener, blacksmith at Bradfield, had made all the preparation for firing the anvil and was just giving the plug a last hard tap to drive it firmly home when the charge exploded and drove the handle of the sledgehammer clear through his body.

Blacksmiths also have a close association with chestnut trees. Everybody knows Longfellow's verse: "Under the spreading chestnut tree, The village smithy stands; The smith, a mighty man is he, With large and sinewy hands ..." In my young days when blacksmiths were still working, I saw smithy and tree together in many different villages. Here is my suggestion of the reason for it. Horseshoes were the blacksmith's bread and butter. In winter, look at the branches of a horse-chestnut where the leaves have fallen off and you will see that the scar reproduces exactly the shape of a horseshoe and the marks where the nails would go.

GREAT TOTHAM

Has it ever happened to you? You have a dream and some time later you have the weird experience of that dream being acted out in real life. What is the explanation? We will never know, but we do know that it has been going on for a very long time. Let me take you back 150 years:

Frederick Cottee and Abraham Petchey were honest workmen, sawyers employed by timber merchant James Cottee at Brick Hall, Great Totham. With one man above and one man below in the sawpit they could reduce the largest Essex oak to a collection of stout planks for onward transport. They were both trustworthy, hard working family men. One morning Abraham came to work with a strange story to tell Fred. In the night he had had a dream that they were both taken ill, died and were buried together. It was a chilling nightmare, but they were both grown men, and in the light of day it was no more than a joke before getting on with the job.

A few days passed and Abraham felt too unwell to go to work. Gradually he got worse and had to take to his bed. Then it was that Fred felt exactly the same pains of which Abraham was complaining. Finally he too was forced to give up work. Both were so ill that, expensive as it was, their wives had to send for the doctor. He did his best according to the limited medical knowledge of the day, but still both men lingered between life and death.

Their employer, James Cottee and his wife did all they could for both families until, after months of increasing debility, Abraham died. He was buried at his

The church of the Holy Innocents, High Beech   *Courtesy Edward Clack*

employer's expense, in Totham chapel yard. Within a fortnight Fred was laid there beside his workmate. They were only 28 and 29 years old. That dream had come true in all its essential details. But the tragedy was compounded in both families, two of Abraham's children and one of Fred's youngsters died at the same time. Everyone in Great Totham was most upset, and for months fear and superstition stopped everyone in that village from telling their friends what their dreams had been the night before.

HIGH BEACH

Of all the noises which assail our long-suffering ears over the weekend none divides people more deeply than bell-ringing. I mean those big bells which hang in the cathedral and in the belfries of village churches all over Essex. These old bells have sounded out through the centuries; in practice during the week, on Sundays in earnest call to Christians to prayer and praise. Then there are the special days like weddings and funerals when joy or sadness are reflected in the music of the bells. It is a melodious din to people who appreciate the long years of British tradition behind them.

Alfred, Lord Tennyson, wrote part of his famous poem, 'In Memoriam' in High Beach churchyard in 1850, with Christmas very much on his mind:

> The time draws near the birth of Christ;
> The moon is hid, the night is still;

The Christmas bells from hill to hill
Answer each other in the night ...
Ring out the old, ring in the new,
Ring, happy bells, across the snow:

The year is going, let him go;
Ring out the false, ring in the true.

There are, however, almost as many people who agree with that other old rhyme:

> Disturbers of the human race,
> Your bells are always ringing,
> I wish your ropes were round your necks,
> And you upon them swinging!

In June, 1840, one Southend vicar, the Reverend Doctor Nolan, got so fed up with the bellringers who regularly woke him up at six in the morning that he dashed out of the vicarage in his pyjamas and rushed up the belfry steps waving a carving knife. He did not intend murder, he just wanted to cut those wretched bellropes.

For my part I still like to hear the Writtle bells in the frosty night air sending out their age-old message of faith and hope.

WIDFORD

It was not all sweetness and light in the Essex countryside a hundred and fifty years ago and here is a true story to prove it. Widow Charlotte Saltwell of Good Easter had walked over to Writtle to visit her daughter on 6th June, 1849, and stayed to lunch with her. Then she set off for Widford and by half past two she was well along Grove Lane. Without the traffic noises which assail our ears today the song of the birds was the only sound to be heard, but then Charlotte picked out another sound - surely it was the cry of a baby? - but there was not a person in sight. She went to the side of the lane from which she thought the cries were coming. She looked across the roadside ditch and through the hedgerow to the field beyond - there was no sign of another human being. Then, as she turned away to resume her journey her eye was caught by the basket with a closed lid which lay in the ditch. That was the source of the cry.

Charlotte was so upset and frightened that she did not dare to retrieve the basket for fear of what she should find. She ran off up the lane as fast as she could, but it was not until she had almost reached Widford Hall that she saw another person, Mrs. Hannah Cooper, who lived down in the village. Breathlessly she gasped out her plea for help and the two of them went back to the place where the baby's screams were certainly making its presence plain. The ditch, though overgrown with nettles, was only shallow, and Hannah Cooper was quick to retrieve the basket and unfasten the lid. The poor baby was really too big for the basket, so its head had been bent to one side to fit it in. Charlotte was quick to take it out of its uncomfortable little prison and found it was wearing a clean night-gown and was lying on a blanket.

They took it to the nearest house, Mr Hammond's, and he gave them food for it. Hannah reckoned it looked half starved. They then called on the Important Local Person - the Overseer of the Poor - and the three of them went off down to the Chelmsford Workhouse in Wood Street, getting there about four-thirty. To cut a long story short, Superintendent May of the county police, 'acting on information received', as they say, traced the baby back to Priscilla Ruffle. She and a non-conformist minister had taken a circuitous journey by train and gig from Woodham Ferrers to get rid of her unwanted, illegitimate child. She went to jail for three months, and the minister for twelve.

CANVEY ISLAND

What a fight you could have seen on Canvey Island in 1857. The old bare-knuckle boxing champion, Ben Caunt, had reigned from 1838 to 1845, then he retired to run a public house, the Coach and Horses in St. Martin's Lane, London. In an argument there over a drink he fell out with his old friend and fellow fighter, Nat Langham, and challenged him to a fight to settle the issue. Ben was then 42 years old and Nat 37, hardly the age for fisticuffs.

This kind of public fighting was already banned by the authorities, so the organisers kept the venue secret until the last possible moment. Trains from London were declared to be going to Southend, but the real train for those in the know left Fenchurch Street for Tilbury. From there a fleet of boats was waiting to sail out into the Thames estuary and then double back to a landing on Canvey Island.

At a quarter past four on 22nd September, 1857, the two men threw their hats into the ring in the formal challenge and then set to. There was no shaking of hands as was usual for this was a grudge match. Caunt dropped Langham in the first round with a left and right to the ribs, but Langham laughed it off and came flailing in again. In the fifty-first round Caunt had a nasty mishap. He swung a wild punch at Langham, missed him altogether but connected painfully with one of the stakes which held the rope marking out the ring. For sixty exhausting rounds they battled - Langham was knocked down in fifty-nine of them, but Caunt never did hit the grass.

When the timekeeper called for the sixtieth round both men were so weary that they could only stand and eye each other while they massaged their bruises. Friends stepped in, persuaded them that they had both had enough, that honours were even and that they should shake hands and be friends again. They agreed, shook hands, and Ben Caunt's last fight was over. They had no friends, though, among the bookmakers and the gamblers round the ring.

It was on Canvey Island that Tom Sayers, claimed by punters to be the greatest champion of all these bare-knuckle bruisers, fought three times in eighteen months from February, 1857. George Caunt writes his epitaph, "Tom Sayers was one of the finest of English fist fighters, but unlike so many of the champions who lived to a ripe old age, he died at the age of thirty-eight, the victim of his own dissipations."

The Lobster Smack, Canvey Island

LOUGHTON

In the second half of the nineteenth century great tracts of the old forest of Epping were literally being stolen by local landowners extending their boundaries, then selling off the land to developers. In 1865 the Lord of the Manor of Loughton enclosed 1,316 acres of the Forest, put a high fence all round it, and started the wholesale felling of trees to make roads for new housing estates. Just one man stood in his way. His name was Thomas Willingale, an ordinary working man with no knowledge of the law. He insisted that he had the ancient right to go into the Forest in winter months and lop off the lower branches of trees for fuel, from which he made a humble living. He would not give up that right.

His sons and his friends supported him. They broke down the fence, were arrested, and got seven days' hard labour for their persistence. One of the magistrates who sentenced them was himself engaged in obtaining forest land for development.

It had been a tradition in the village of Loughton from time immemorial that at midnight between 10th and 11th November, which is St. Martin's day, all the poorer folk would carry out their lopping ritual to preserve their right, have a barrel of beer beside a big bonfire, then haul home their winter fuel. Thomas was simply following that tradition, and he found help from people of influence and wealth who saw the wickedness that was being perpetrated. Lawyers helped him take his case to the Master of the Rolls. It was fully reported on 6th March, 1866, under the headline FOREST RIGHTS and won Thomas national acclaim for his dogged refusal to give up his right to wander in the Forest and collect his kindling. The poor old man died before the case was settled gloriously in his favour. The Corporation of the City of London lent its weight in favour of the Forest, bought out all the owners of Forest land and helped to frame the Epping Forest Act which was passed in 1880.

The icing on the cake was that Queen Victoria travelled into Epping Forest on 6th May, 1882, to declare it a public open space for ever. We could say that it was at the cost of £250,000 to the City of London and half the life of Thomas Willingale.

LITTLE HORKESLEY

Love is a quality hard to define. Let me offer my interpretation in the form of a true story. In 1866 a baby girl was born out of wedlock to a woman who was no more than a girl herself. The baby was left with its grandparents at Little Horkesley while her mother carried on her job as servant in a big house in London. The baby grew up adoring her grandparents whom she always thought of as Mum and Dad. As a young girl she also went into service with a Colchester family, but she kept in touch with her family and friends at Little Horkesley, where she was held in the greatest affection.

When the Bourdillons at Little Horkesley Hall heard that she had fallen ill they paid for her to go into a London hospital and get expert attention. Now her real mother, who had since married a kind-hearted cabinet-maker called Joseph Ball, could visit her long-lost daughter, to tell her the truth of her birth and the circumstances which forced her to leave her in her grandmother's care. Sadly, it became evident that the poor girl was too ill to be cured and she herself realised this. She so wanted to get back home and implored Joseph and her mother to see that when she died she would be buried in the place where she had had such a happy childhood. Her stepfather, touched and saddened, solemnly promised that she should.

That was not an easy promise to keep. When the poor girl died Joseph found he did not have enough money to pay for a coffin, let alone the cost of its transport by rail all the way to north Essex - but he did not hesitate. He borrowed enough money from a friend to buy some timber and made a coffin himself. He took it round to the hospital on a handcart, collected his stepdaughter's body and forthwith set out for Little Horkesley on foot, facing a journey of sixty miles. Feeble from illness himself he still pressed on, stopping over-night at Ingatestone and Witham, and he reached at last at his wife's old home.

Such extraordinary devotion and determination based on a love which had hardly had time to flower reached the ears of journalists. I am glad to say that a fund was raised to help Joseph cover all his costs and see him safely back to his wife and home.

The 1412 brass of Sir Thomas Swynborne, Little Horkesley

51

COLCHESTER

There is one thing you will never see again, and that is a travelling menagerie. In those had old days from 1850 to the last war anybody who had not been to a circus was a nobody - and the menagerie was the collection of animals trained to excite and amuse the public. In 1870 a huge advertisement appeared in the local papers to announce that Edmond's, late Wombwell's, Royal Windsor Castle and Crystal Palace Menagerie would be stopping for a night at Colchester, Kelvedon, Witham, Great Waltham, Chelmsford, Maldon, Rayleigh and Southend on a summertime tour.

In those days the human attitude to animals was different. People curious about the world around them would never see these creatures from parts of the world they could never visit, so they flocked in their hundreds to the menagerie made up of cages brought down the bumpy high road by a slow procession of horses and elephants and drawn up in the Fair Field or even in the town market place. Since the camera was still then an expensive novelty the menagerie was their only chance to see such wonders.

The advertisement offered 'The Umbrella Elephants', the 'Great White Camel', a baby camel and lion cubs only a few weeks old, 'Fire-hoop Braving Hyenas', leopards and lemurs, wombats and zebras. The biggest attraction was a pair of rhinos brought over from India specially that very year. The poor creatures had to perform in one way or another three times daily, with the last performance at 9 p.m. Admission was a shilling [5p], quite a sum in those days, and you had to pay an extra sixpence if you wanted to see the animals feeding in their cages afterwards.

Even then though, there were some doubts expressed, if we read between the lines: "... the animals, or most of them, seem as happy as possible." But let us remember also that the marvelling folk of yesteryear did not have the benefit of colour television to bring the wonders of the world into their very homes.

BARKINGSIDE

Long before the octopus of London grabbed bits of Essex in its tentacles Barkingside was a charming hamlet tucked away in the countryside north of Ilford. A guidebook brought out a hundred years ago tells us of its most important building: "Here is Dr. Barnado's Village Home for Destitute Girls. The inmates, numbering about 600, are accommodated in 30 separate houses arranged in a square. Others are in the course of erection. The matrons are chiefly ladies who voluntarily give their services." That shows how famous these homes had become in a mere eight years, for they started as four cottages built in 1873 in what might be called the back garden of Mossford Lodge, within walking distance of today's Gants Hill roundabout.

Dr. Thomas John Barnado, born in 1845, was only seventeen when he made the decision to spend his life helping less fortunate people. He was only 22 when he founded his East End Mission for Destitute

Children in 1867. He toured the East End, picking up waifs who had no home but the pavement and gave them a new life of hope and happiness. In 1870 he opened his Boys' Home at Stepney Causeway. When he was given Mossford Lodge as a wedding present he had part of it adapted to house 60 girls. That was in 1873 and within six years 24 cottage homes had been built in the grounds.

When the good man died in 1905, 1,300 girls were being brought up in 64 cottages spread around the Lodge's 300 acres. Taking them together with the boys home it has been reckoned that, in his lifetime, Dr. Barnado was directly responsible for the rescue and loving care of at least 250,000 children. His ashes are buried in the Children's Church of his famous village under a single, dignified monument designed by Sir George Frampton. His life's work is summed up by his own simple remark - "I have never seen an ugly child."

Charles Dickens pointed up the plight of the children of the poor in our larger towns in novels which woke the national conscience. Dr. Thomas Barnado did better - he let that conscience stir him to personal action and his example led at last to a national effort which now looks to the principle of the individual fostering of deprived children in people's own homes.

SANDON

We walk about the beautiful country lanes and footpaths of Essex, admiring the scenery in places which look so serene, quite unaware of the darker side of life lurking below the surface, known only to the old inhabitants and handed down in family lore. Take Sandon for example, a village where nothing seems to have happened since Cardinal Wolsey built that beautiful church tower more than four hundred years ago.

In 1870 John Finch had been a regular worshipper at that church, but he changed abruptly to the sect of the `Peculiar People'. He was known in the village as a man of low intelligence and unstable character who worked as an agricultural labourer for John Bures, farmer, at Sandon Hall. He lived with his wife and family in one of a row of three cottages in Woodhill Road, half a mile from the church. Walk there of a summer Sunday evening in the peace of the place and you would never believe the terrible thing that happened in that cottage bedroom. On 26th May, 1870, John Finch was up as early as ever, but he knew his wife would never rise again. Yet, as usual he called his eldest child, a ten-year-old girl to get up and then called up to his wife, "Mother, are you dressing?". He and she shared a room with a four-year-old girl and a six-month-old baby, while the other three children slept in the second room.

Without another word John went off up the road. The girl he had called got up, could not do up her dress, went into her mother's bedroom to ask for help - and found her mother lying in bed covered with blood and unable to speak. The little girl ran round to her neighbour Mrs. Crow, who saw a scene so frightful that she could not enter the room. She sent for Mr Devenish, the wheelwright, who found Mrs. Finch dead from the most awful gashes about her face and neck. The baby, covered in blood, lay uninjured in its mother's arms.

They sent for the village constable. He found a blood-stained hedging bill or chopper and caught up with Finch out in the fields. He seemed to have no idea of the enormity of his crime. At his trial the jury took no time at all to return a verdict of not guilty 'on the ground that the prisoner was of unsound mind at the time he committed the act'. The judge then committed poor John Finch 'to be kept under proper care during Her Majesty's pleasure'.

CASTLE HEDINGHAM

Hedingham Castle is a lovely place to visit, to picnic on its lawns and to step back a thousand years with those ancient walls as a backdrop for so many dramas. At the same time we should spare a thought for a man who lived in a cottage in the shadow of that castle keep where his father had set up a small pottery. That man was Edward Bingham: in that pottery he played with clay as most of us play with plasticine. In that rural paradise in the middle of the last century Edward roamed the countryside, fascinated by the plant and animal life which had such an influence on his wood carving and clay modelling.

He tried striking out on his own, but he was soon back helping his father in the pottery, turning out also a few of his own very individual pieces, with much coloured and moulded decoration. They caught the eye in amongst his father's plain garden pottery pieces and were often purchased by the casual visitor. After he had taken over altogether from his ageing father Edward came across a book on the life of the great potter Wedgwood, which inspired him to improve his own work. The better quality of these pots, with the unusual decorations in blues, greens and browns brought orders from wholesalers far beyond the county boundary.

In 1876 his pottery was the subject of a visit by the Essex Archæological Society and, charmed by their primitive vigour, the members bought many pots. Edward Bingham had reached his 'Golden Age'. By 1885 he had thirteen kilns in operation, when the *Essex County Chronicle* said of the pottery shed: "The walls and beams seem every inch of them to be covered with texts of scripture having references to potters and pottery roughly written in chalk or on slips of paper." There is no doubt Edward was an eccentric with a sense of humour. In some of the mugs he made he put a frog, modelled in clay, inside, at the bottom. You didn't see the frog until you had drunk your beer. And when our Edward got fed up with making pots in Hedingham what do you think he did? - He emigrated to America - at the age of 87.

KELVEDON

This is a believe-it-or-not story about a French dog's adventure in Essex. It was of the breed they called *Braque du Pays*, a close relation of the English pointer. A prime example of its breed, it had won the gold medal at the Paris International Exhibition's dog show in 1878. Its owner sent it over to England to offer it at stud to any English dog breeder who wished to improve the English breed at Dr. Salter's kennels in Tolleshunt D'Arcy. Although he was the much-loved and respected doctor for an area stretching from Tiptree to the banks of the Blackwater he still found time for dog-breeding, showing and racing and was an acknowledged authority in the world of dogs.

Dr J H Salter, JP, MRCS

This dog, called Kermes, arrived safely by train at Kelvedon station in crate which was left on the platform there to be picked up by Dr. Salter. An express train rushed through the station with such an explosion of noise and speed that Kermes broke out the side of his crate, leapt on to the railway track and was quickly lost to sight in the distance. When he discovered this disaster Dr. Salter was very upset. He had paid a high fee to have the dog on loan - what would it cost him now to replace it? His breeding programme was in tatters.

He went down on the next slow train and left a message with every stationmaster to keep a look-out for Kermes. Then he notified the police locally and nationally and put advertisements in all the papers and the doggy periodicals. Weeks went by, but not a word was heard of a pointer-like dog dead or alive in the district. Then, one day on the train, Dr. Salter fell into conversation with a fellow passenger who told him that a blacksmith at Bradwell-on-Sea had rescued a dog in a distressed condition which he thought must have come out of the water from a sinking ship.

The doctor followed up this remote lead and found to his delight that the dog was indeed Kermes. He postulated that it had set out for France with a strong homing instinct just as soon as it cleared the station, and coming to the bank of the estuarine Blackwater, where it was about two miles wide, it plunged in, and swam for France but came ashore, most fortunately, at Bradwell where it was hardly able to crawl. This must surely be the father of all shaggy dog stories.

MALDON

I cannot imagine that we will ever see again a man the like of Sir Claude Champion de Crespigny. Not in our green, self-righteous present land. Sir Claude was a sportsman who would chase anything that moved; give him a horse and he would race anything that moved. He risked his life in every sphere of adventurous activity. At Champion Lodge, recovering from a badly broken leg caused in a ballooning accident at Maldon, he found time to put together notes for his book *Forty Years of a Sportsman's Life*, which was published privately in 1910. But for one of his most amazing adventures we have to go to the account of a Meet at Champion Lodge on 19th February, 1881, recalled by A. W. Ruggles-Brise.

It was a cold, misty, damp day, made worse by a bitter east wind. The Hunt moved off to Totham, thirty hunters and the yelping pack. They started a fox which ran and ran. By the time it had led them down through Goldhanger to the Tolleshunt Beckingham marshes and the salt water of a full tide only three or four men were still in the hunt. The wily fox took to the open water and made it to a small island three hundred yards out in what could be called open water. Up comes one of the gentlemen, in a green coat and a hunting cap. "Here, take this," he said, throwing down his hunting cap and coat, and with a cheer to the hounds to follow him, he leapt head first into the water, followed by half a dozen hounds. "It was our worthy baronet, Sir Claude de Crespigny. It was all done in a moment,

Sir Claude de Crespigny

with marvellous pluck and an undaunted love of adventure ... With breathless anxiety we looked on, fearing the cold and cramp might affect the bold baronet. But he was always possessed of nine lives, with an outstanding vitality. Presently he gained the island, and a scuffle took place between the hounds and the fox, and all went into the water. The hounds got back on the island, but no fox. But it was not all over, for, to our amazement, we saw the baronet diving, and to our joy and wonder he came up, holding the fox aloft. Was ever there such a hunting scene? Or will there ever be such again?"

BATTLESBRIDGE

In the dense, black foggy night of 24th January, 1882, Samuel Cripps, mail cart driver, set out for Chelmsford where he was to pick up the mail for Rochford, Southend and all the villages on his way. He got to Chelmsford safely, loaded the cart with the bags of mail and, at two o'clock in the morning, set out on the trip back to Southend. Still the fog persisted, reducing visibility to no more than a few yards but the horse plodded on and everything went well as far as Battlesbridge, then horse and driver lost their sense of direction in the fog. Where the road turned abruptly to run along by Mr. Meeson's millpond part of the brick wall which guarded the road from the river had given way and fallen into the water, leaving a wide gap. In the fog the horse headed for it as if it was the clear way ahead. There came a sudden, terrible drop into sixteen feet of icy, winter water. Samuel Cripps went flying head over heels off the cart and down to bottom of the millpond.

Self-preservation certainly concentrates the mind. Samuel came up, found the mail cart, clambered on top of it, and was able to stand with his head just above the water. He found the whistle which every mailman carried, blew it with all the breath he had left, and shouted for dear life. Two workmen, up early to get to their work heard his cries and traced his whereabouts in the fog. With great presence of mind Samuel remembered that in his pocket he had a rope, for securing items of mail. He tied one end round his arm and threw the other end to the men who were able to grab it and so bring him to the bank in a totally exhausted state.

Half the village of Battlesbridge were up by this time and willing helpers got the poor horse out, along with the mail cart. The horse, half-drowned and badly injured, died soon afterwards, but Samuel, taken to the house of Mr. Pitts, the sub-postmaster was massaged vigorously to restore his circulation, and put to bed. The mail bags had floated some three miles down the River Crouch but they were all recovered, dried out at Rochford and eventually each letter was delivered, with apologies. The man who suffered most loss was the fellow who had contracted with the Post Office to collect and deliver the mail. He had to have the cart repaired and buy a new horse!

SOUTHEND

Very early on a Monday morning, a cold January day in 1888, long before it was light, the fishing smack *Conqueror* had turned for home way out by the Girdle lightship off Southend. The light on its stout mast was still shining out its intermittent signal, but the captain of the *Emmanuel*, a coaster bound from Stockton to the Port of London, heavily laden with a general cargo was not keeping a look-out. Its captain did not see how close he was to the *Conqueror* either and, despite warning cries from the fishermen, the *Emmanuel* crashed into the smack, slicing it right through to the mast. It began to sink very rapidly. Let its owner, Mr. Myall, carry on the story: "Realising our position, I, my son, and Herbert Wright, three out of the crew of four, at once made for the skiff and jumped in, just in time, as the smack disappeared in the very cold sea. We were extremely anxious as to our mate, Robert Cotgrove, for we feared that he was down in the hold. We called and shouted for him until we were hoarse as we rowed about in the vicinity of the vessel, but we could neither see nor hear anything of him."

Poor fellows, there was nothing more they could do. The steamboat had stopped some distance ahead, and the fishermen, soaked to the skin and shivering with cold, rowed over to it and were helped aboard. Imagine their surprise and their relief when they saw their shipmate Bob Cotgrove waiting to greet them with a big smile on his face. He told them he was up for'ard when he had seen the steamer coming for them out of the darkness, so he had shinned up the rigging as quickly as he could, and when the *Emmanuel* struck the *Conqueror* he stepped straight out of the rigging on to the steamer's deck - much to the surprise of the unwatchful crew.

The captain of the *Emmanuel* confessed that he did not know where he was so Mr. Myall showed him the light-ship's beam still flashing faintly in the dawn and pointed him in the right direction. At five o'clock in the morning the castaways were landed at Southend pier. As Mr. Myall said after he had recovered from the ordeal, "Although I have had some narrow escapes from drowning in my time, I don't think I ever was so near it as I was on this occasion."

Southend pier head, 1890. *Painting by W L Wyllie*

58

CHELMSFORD

When Chelmsford was granted its charter as a Borough in 1888 the celebrations included the decoration of their houses by the townspeople. The house of Mr. Edmund Durrant was declared to be the second best in originality and artistry. But few people know who Ed Durrant was or why he is worth remembering today. He was a Chelmsford man through and through, born there in February, 1843.

He went to the Grammar School and then worked for Hatchard's, the London booksellers, to gain experience before he bought up Burrell's, the Chelmsford bookseller at 90, High Street. He went on to develop the local history side of the business and soon became active in the literary interest then positively buzzing in the town, including the improvement of the Chelmsford Museum of which he was for many years the Secretary. He was also a leader in the continuing campaign for a town library, but did not live to see the magnificent building erected in 1906 to house both library and museum.

In 1888 Ed founded his own Literary Society under the name of `Chelmsford Odde Volumes'. It was limited to just 49 `Odde Volumes' who, on pain of a fine, had to address fellow members only by the volume number given them on joining. What a select band of Chelmsfordians they were. They met at Ed's house in the High Street and they wandered all over Essex in their quest of art, architecture, science and local history. The minutes of their meetings are still preserved in the local history collection in Chelmsford Library where you can also read Edmund Durrant's own *Reminiscences of Old Chelmsford*.

He died in 1900 and his obituary concludes, "How very many will miss a kind friend and courteous tradesman may be shown at the quiet funeral ... when the remains were laid to rest of one who was essentially an Essex man, although never so prominent as he might have been had his modesty been less ... May it be long before his memory is forgotten ..." Who remembers dear old Ed Durrant today? There are all sorts of blue plaques about the town commemorating people far less important in the history of Chelmsford, and certainly far less full of fun and friendship than Mr. Edmund Durrant.

BRAINTREE

Doctor John Harrison was probably the most popular doctor Braintree ever had. He was born at Bocking on 11th July, 1857, and educated at Felsted School. He was also a great practical joker who became the bane of his family and friends. Take, for instance, the night he was drinking with friends at the White Hart in Braintree. He spotted a Shalford builder and undertaker refreshing himself rather liberally after attending the Braintree Wednesday market. He had one more call to make - a coffin to deliver which was loaded on his trap in the stables behind the inn. `Doctor John' as he was known by all, had spotted that coffin and saw the makings of a little joke. He quietly spread the word among his friends and they all saw that the builder always had a drink at

High Street, Braintree, 1895

his elbow, When he became too tipsy even to keep awake they helped him out to the stable and into the coffin where he fell deeply asleep. They harnessed the horse, gave it a slap on the flank and away it went up the street, homeward bound on its familiar regular journey. But what a shock it must have been to the builder's family to hear the trap come back, to look for him and find him in that coffin.

One of Dr. John's neighbours in Bank Street was Frank Crittall. In an election in the 1890's they supported opposing parties. The Doctor, campaigning for the 'blue' Conservative faction, lured Frank's son, six-year-old Valentine, into his house, rigged him all out in blue, even dyed his face and hands and took him round the town in his trap while he canvassed votes. Frank Crittall of the 'yellow' liberal persuasion thought this was really going too far and got his own back. In the dead of night he and his friends, quiet as mice, painted the front of the Doctor's house, windows, doors and even the step itself a loud and vivid yellow. They still stayed friends.

One rich old lady, a hypochondriac, was always ringing the worthy doctor in the middle of the night to get him to go and see her. He knew that there was really nothing wrong with her when he got a call in the night after a very tiring day at the Newmarket races, where he put on his other coat as a bookmaker. So he told his patient that there was only one rare medicine that would cure her and that he would have to drive through the night to London for it. He went back to bed, had a good sleep, then took her round a harmless bottle of medicine he had made up on spot - and charged a huge fee for this special attention.

STEBBING

Sometimes you can come across a newspaper account which makes you smile, the anecdote itself, the quaintness of language in which it is expressed or even in the strangeness of some of the names of the characters themselves. Take, for example, the story of that New Year's Day a hundred years ago when the Braintree millwright Charles Chopping made a fool of himself in the Red Lion at Stebbing. He ended up in most uncomfortable custody in Dunmow's police cell for nine days until he could be taken to appear at Dunmow Police Court. There the magistrates got a full account of his misdemeanour. They heard Esther Crow, a sixteen-year-old servant girl, say that Charlie had followed her into the parlour - and made an improper suggestion. Later that same evening he caught hold of her apron as she passed by and tried to pull her on to his lap. He didn't appear to be drunk, she said, but when Joseph Barker wouldn't stand his round and buy him a tankard of ale, Charlie took the kettle off the fire in the tap room and flung its contents over Barker's knees.

The next witness to the night's events was Alfred Sycamore, the landlord. He told the magistrates how he grabbed and held Charlie while someone ran for the police, who arrived in the daunting shape of P.C. Bright. So poor old Charlie, a bit tiddly on New Year's Day, had overstepped the mark - and the magistrates were not a bit sympathetic. For flirting with Esther, the darling of the Red Lion, he was sentenced to six weeks' hard labour - and that was in the days when it really did mean strictly supervised very hard work. For throwing the hot water over Joseph Barker he had to serve an extra two weeks' hard labour; there was none of that nonsense about concurrent sentences in those days. As for Mr. Sycamore, the Bench told him, "You did your duty," and he was freed from the worry that he might lose his licence.

What made me smile? Look at the names. A Sycamore stood up to a Chopping who wanted to catch a Crow and got his own back on an old dog called Barker who got into a lot of hot water. And the name of one of the magistrates who had Chopping clapped in jail? - Dr. Clapham!

BOCKING

Should children be punished physically, at home or at school? Educators and social workers should take heart; many experts and parents before them have been unable to square this particular circle. A century ago Frank Smith, headmaster of Bocking Board School, landed up in court over the treatment of one of his pupils.

It started like this; eleven-year-old Frank Dowsett was a regular little termagant. One of his difficulties was that he could not, or would not listen to what he was being told. So, when it came to writing on his slate the answers to questions on what he had learned he was constantly looking at his neighbours' slates for inspiration. Five times did Mr. Smith chide him for this. On 1st July, 1893, he did it again, and so, in desperation, Mr. Smith hauled him to the front of the class and gave him a couple of strokes of the cane on each hand. It stung, but it did not hurt too much so he put on a brave front and told another boy, Arthur Arnold, that old Smithy ought to have his cane taken away and he should get a good caning.

He told the wrong boy. Young Arnold split on him to Mr. Smith. He ordered him to write on his slate exactly what Frank Dowsett had said and said he would deal with him on the following Monday. Hearing this from the virtuous tell-tale Frank put on a swagger. Picking up a stone, he said he would throw it at the headmaster if he tried to cane him again. He took that stone to school with him on the Monday and as the master took up his cane Frank threw it at him, hitting him on the hand. This was rank mutiny. Mr. Smith

ordered two boys to hold him, by the legs and the back of his neck, and, without taking down his knickerbockers, gave him several hard strokes of the cane.

When he got home with his sad tale his mother put on her coat and took her boy to two of the school governors and on to the doctor, to show them the bruises inflicted. Then she took the headmaster to court, where the doctor described the four bruises he had seen on the boy's bottom. The headmaster's solicitor said, "I daresay, Doctor, you have had the same thing when you were about the same age?" - "I have had a good many," - "And you are alive to tell the tale?" - "I still exist, of course." The outcome was that the case was dismissed. I hope that spanking taught the boy to respect authority - and to keep his own counsel.

Church Street, Bocking, 1905

62

MALDON

Maldon has a `believe it or not' feature seldom seen by tourists, and largely unknown to its inhabitants. As you approach the town along London Road you will see a turning on the left labelled Dykes Chase. Look on the other side of that road and you will see a sign clearly saying it is Lodge Road. Only the narrowest strip of weed-grown land serves to establish that these are separate roads with their own identity. How could two streets have been made so close together about a century ago?

The whole story is based on the court case of *Gozzett v. Maldon Corporation*, heard in January, 1894. It began like this: in July, 1892, Mr. P. M. Beaumont bought the Lodge estate, but not the actual house called the Lodge. His first step in developing the land was to close the original drive and make a new private road on the northwest side, fifteen feet wide, closed by gates at each end, so that it was strictly private. There was just one special person to whom he granted a right of way and that was Mr. Gozzett, who had bought the Lodge and a small part of its garden.

Then Mr. Beaumont leased part of the front garden with a right of way over that road to the far end, a distance of 170 feet. Then he divided out the remainder of the garden he owned into building plots which he offered for sale. Meanwhile, Mr. Gozzett was planning to build two houses on his own ground right next to Mr. Beaumont's. He put his plans to the council, but they said he could not do it because the road already planned by Mr.

Beaumont did not reach the required minimum of 36 feet for houses each side. Mr. Gozzett ignored their refusal and began digging the foundations for his houses with his own road literally touching Mr. Beaumont's. So he ended up in court charged with laying out a new street, which he had named Lodge Road, contrary to the byelaws.

He contended that all he had ever wanted to do was to build two houses on the ground he owned and that Lodge Road still had its gates at each end, was only open to traffic to and from the Lodge residence, so it was still a private road. The judges came down on his side, the case was quashed and the council had to pay the costs, so the road with two names remains to this day.

John Robert Bourne was worth a lot of money when he died in his house in Wantz Road, Maldon, in 1894. He was a bachelor, aged 78, who had been confined to his bed for eight years and was looked after by Miss Bond, his housekeeper and only companion through more than twenty years. He had always lived modestly, never advertising his wealth in any way, in clothing, food or drink.

He kept a lot of money in the house, some four to five thousand pounds in notes and gold - half a million by today's values. For years he had kept it, most uncomfortably I should think, under his pillow, to guard against theft, then he was persuaded by his housekeeper to keep it all in a box in a cupboard right next to his bed. It should said he did also have two considerable bank accounts, so he was hedging his bets. He trusted Miss Bond implicitly.

One day, needing some small change, she called in a boy from the street and sent him round to the Star Inn, almost next door with a note which she wanted changed into cash. The landlady looked at it, said she did not have enough cash handy to pay it, and sent the lad back. Miss Bond told the lad to try the baker. Mrs. Filbey, the landlady, saw the lad a day or two later and asked him if he had been able to get the note changed. The boy said he had, the baker had given him the £5 in cash. Mrs. Filbey was horrified, and told him that the note was actually for £500. She went round to the baker, who said he had barely looked at it as he put it in his pocket-book. It was returned to Miss Bond, and he got his £5 back.

John Bourne had few relatives. The landed property, worth in our day some £800,000, went to Mrs. Rayner, widow of a Braintree farmer, while John Bourne's distant relatives, the Wood family of Southend, who admitted that they had hardly ever heard of him, let alone spoken to him, received one eighteenth of his estate. Another highly delighted beneficiary was his brother's widow, for she had been working for several years to support herself as a charwoman at Maldon's King's Head Hotel. The rumour went round the town that included in all the money found in John Bourne's bedroom was a sackful of spade guineas.

Maldon *Courtesy Essex County Newspapers*

CHELMSFORD

Chelmsford lost the chance to make its mark in history as the home of a most remarkable mechanical marvel - the steam omnibus. The man who pioneered this 'dinosaur' of modern bus travel was Thomas Clarkson who had been looking for suitable premises in an ever-spreading circle round London, when he lighted on the factory site in Anchor Street, Chelmsford, which Colonel Crompton had occupied until his Anchor Works were burned down in the disastrous fire of 1895. It was fortunate that T. H. P. Dennis had kept his foundry going on part of the site, for a foundry was one of Thomas's first requirements.

Now he was able to put all his theoretical workings to the test in the production of a prototype steam omnibus which he called the 'Chelmsford', which he described as " ... a substantial, roomy steam brougham suitable for the conveyance in comfort of eight passengers with their luggage over long journeys." He was really just too late with his idea, for the petrol-driven internal combustion engine was taking over, despite steam's reliability and power. There was hope though, for at one of his demonstrations a group of Torquay businessmen developing a local bus service asked Thomas if he could alter his design to take more people. In a matter of weeks he had a new model drawn up and accepted. It was put into

Clarkson's demonstration bus, registration number F2582, outside the White Hart, Chelmsford in 1908

Two National Bus Company Clarkson steam buses, destinations Coggeshall and Colchester

production in Chelmsford and the first one was driven out of the works and straight down to Exeter where the purchasers were picked up for their trial run down to Torquay. It arrived in perfect working order, and won him a contract for eight more, all of which he had delivered by early in 1905. A letter by a 'Regular Reader' to the *Torquay Times* declared that the "bus'... is a huge success and is much appreciated," and adding that, as it ran along the coast road at the height of a storm, "It was quite a treat to see the bus charge the waves, which broke over it as high as a three-storey house."

Buses with 'Chelmsford' proudly blazoned on their side went into service in India, New Zealand and Barbados. Yet at this time it was not in service in its home town. It was a dinosaur, beautifully built, but out of its time and there is nothing left in Chelmsford now to mark its passing.

WOODHAM FERRERS

Folk at South Woodham Ferrers are rather proud of their new town while the ancient village of Woodham Ferrers to the north wraps its old coat round its ageing limbs and looks back with quiet satisfaction through a history of more than a thousand years - hiding a ninety-year-old secret of violence and intrigue.

You would think that a candidate's public meeting in an election campaign would be a pretty dull affair in such a tiny, out-of-the-way village. The Liberal agent had arranged just such a meeting on a Saturday evening at the end of September, 1900 - one of dozens in his constituency. But a young headstrong gang of anti-Liberals planned their own campaign, and we have an on-the-spot account of what happened:

"... Owing to the turbulence of some young men, the whole meeting was completely upset, and it was impossible for the speakers, who hailed from Chelmsford, to proceed. The local constable advised a postponement, and this was agreed to, but as the party were driving back to Chelmsford the young fellows in question attacked them from behind the corner of a hedge, pelting them with rotten eggs and bags of flour." The newspaper reporter takes up the story: "It is also alleged that missiles of a far more dangerous nature were hurled at the Liberals ... Mr. George Smith of Chelmsford, was hit in the eye and injured by a bag of flour containing a stone, necessitating a visit to a doctor. His ...se was also cut."

Three other Liberals ran the gauntlet and were "besmeared with flour and rotten eggs, and they arrived home in a sorry plight." Not only that - these bad lads placed their bicycles together in the hedge so that their lights blazed directly into the faces of the horses drawing the Liberals' traps, not only to frighten the horses but also to light up the targets for their projectiles. The rather righteous reporter concluded: "Such behaviour as this should be sternly discountenanced."

A new meeting was held the following Wednesday and the pro-Liberal villagers turned up with cudgels and sticks but, typical of our good old English way of life, nothing happened at all.

OSEA ISLAND

Osea, in the Blackwater estuary east of Maldon, was at one time a home for alcoholics, where they could stay to 'dry out', hopefully to return to their loved ones as cured, reformed, teetotallers. The island had been bought by N. F. Charrington, of the well-known brewing family. He had become so upset at the damage alcoholic addiction was doing to families of all classes that he sold out his interest in the family firm for around a million pounds and set about projects like the purchase of this little Essex island on which he had erected buildings to accommodate and support a stream of alcoholics from the poorer districts of London. It was started in 1903 and by the following January it was reported that the work was 'steadily developing, and promises to do so more rapidly when the unemployed are set to work on the island. An inebriates' home is being built by Dr. Moore, of Hastings, and arrangements are being made for the erection of an East-end Convalescent Home as well. As far as possible, Mr. Charrington wants to make the place an old-fashioned village. There is to be the village inn - of course, without intoxicants - and buildings will be grouped around. In the eastern part of the island, which has a coastline of over four miles, the natural beauties will remain undisturbed'.

The project got off to a good start, but there were one or two alcoholic hiccups in its progress. One of them was caused by Henry Lawrence, a scaffolder, sent by the Lord Mayor of London's Mansion House Committee to work on the island. On Boxing Day, 1903, he left the island as soon as the tide left the causeway uncovered and went to watch a football match in Maldon. The away team included some old friends. With them he got very drunk, sentimental about his family back home and altogether fed up with his rotten Christmas. At ten thirty on that Saturday night he ended up outside the Maldon home of Charrington's agent for work on Osea. Holding him responsible for his present unhappiness he banged the man's door, asked for the money for his fare back to London and showed him four large stones which would go through his windows if he did not cough up. Poor, drunken, old Henry - he ended up in jail for seven days because he had no means to pay the fine and costs of 7s.6d. [37½p] for disturbing the peace.

The causeway to Osea Island

68

HIGHWOOD

Imagine the peace and quiet in Highwood some ninety years ago. It is still hardly big enough to be called a village - on the road from Writtle to Blackmore. One of its hamlets is called Loves Green; not an appropriate site for a battle - and a battle between two women at that.

It all happened on a summer's evening in August, near the Green Man. Widow Atkins, having partaken of one beer too many loudly proclaimed her challenge - to fight the best woman in Highwood. Without waiting for an answer she picked on Elizabeth Oddy, even though her husband was with her. "She hit me three times," said Elizabeth, "Knocking me into the hedge and giving me a black eye." This was said in court, a fortnight later, when Elizabeth summoned Alice Atkins for assault. The Clerk to the Court said to Elizabeth, "She must have thought you were the best woman in Highwood." Of course, this retort raised a lot of laughter, but Elizabeth was still feeling aggrieved and replied, "She might have done. When I was in the middle of the ditch she kicked me and pulled all this hair out," - showing the magistrates definite bald patches - "Whatever made her do it I don't know. She had just had a row with a young woman. If you asked me I should say she was dead drunk."

At this point the two parties fell to arguing, with the magistrates apparently bemused, and not a little amused. Alice came back at Elizabeth, "Didn't you throw a quartern loaf at me?" - "No!" "Didn't you knock me down twice?" - "No!'

Dramatically Alice produced a blood-stained blouse, and a tooth, which she averred Elizabeth had knocked out. "That was only in self defence," replied Elizabeth. So Alice tried again: "Didn't your husband say he would back you agin any woman in Highwood for £20?" "It's false," was the answer. Then Elizabeth's husband joined in.

"She nearly made my wife bald. When I rebuked her she grazed my face with a stone." Alice responded, "There was no difference between us."

Elizabeth's daughter-in-law put it in a nutshell: "When I went down the lane I saw two women fighting like men. There was no difference between 'em; n'er a one of 'em was sober." Alice was bound over to keep the peace for a year and had to pay four shillings costs. What a way to get your name in the paper.

SOUTH WOODHAM FERRERS

Such strange things went on in South Woodham Ferrers in the days when this hamlet out in the fields was an unlikely mix of smallholders, retired East Enders who put up their own shacks, and young commuters to London employment. At the turn of the century many an honest cockney bought a bit of land at one of the hotel auctions where free drink and a dinner made everybody optimistic. Horace Mudd had done just that, but he ran into trouble in 1905 when he built a little verandah to improve his do-it-yourself home. On completion he looked at it and saw that, by enclosing that verandah he could turn it into two handy little rooms. Someone must have told the Chelmsford Rural District Council, who checked and found that he had not asked them for permission or deposited the requisite plans, and his work did not come up to the standards of their bye-laws. He would not remove it so they had to take him to court.

The Council's solicitor said they were happy for Mr. Mudd to make a proper job of it, or to strip it back to the verandah it had been: he said if they would lend him the money he would deposit plans and make it abide by the laws. But no council can be blackmailed; Mr. Mudd had to pay fines and costs of 18s.0d.. He refused and was sent to prison. When he came out some of the villagers organised a protest meeting which brought down to Woodham a reporter from a London paper, who wrote: "The 'village Grantham' [he meant village Hampden], the victim of bye-law tyranny, pale and weak after his incarceration, told his story to the meeting in broken accents: "Many of you have seen me in my garden in my working dress, but in Springfield Prison I was in sackcloth and arrows ... but I have not lost my determination to fight the Chelmsford Rural District Council about my verandah. I have not taken it down and I will not take it down ... I will not obey this absurd bye-law." He was cheered to the echo and the meeting passed a resolution asking that the Council should be more considerate in future.

To be fair, the newspaper also explained the Council's position. Horace Mudd fought on, taking his case to his M.P. and on to the Home Secretary, but he did not get support. So he dismantled his rooms, the verandah stayed, and he got his own back by renaming his little house "Bye-law Cottage.

TOLLESHUNT D'ARCY

There is an apple unique to Essex, but there is not much chance of buying it in a greengrocer's, even in the county. It is called the D'Arcy Spice apple and it is quite amazing how much local people differ in their accounts of its origin. One person declared that the first tree was found growing in a hedgerow as a 'sport' from unknown parents, somewhere in Tolleshunt D'Arcy. She added that though it grows in an area from Braintree to Burnham, the further it is from its home village, the poorer the quality, and the apple should be left on the tree until long after the frosts and picked only on gaining that characteristic yellow colour.

Another native reckoned that the D'Arcy Spice began as a seedling grown in a load of ballast dumped by a ship that came from the continent; that it was now growing from Colchester down to Maldon, that it should be picked on Guy Fawkes Day and eaten from Boxing Day onwards when it was sweet and juicy for all its murky coloured, withered skin. The third person is probably the one to be believed for her father was gardener to Mr. Binney at Guisnes Court, Tollesbury, around 1906, and told her this story when she was a girl.

One day Dr. Salter, the district's much loved G.P., came over from Tolleshunt to see his old friend and brought with him the first cuttings from his own D'Arcy Spice tree which he had found growing in his garden. He watched the gardener graft them there and then and gave him a cutting for his own garden. The gardener brought it on and from it came the cuttings which he generously distributed far and wide. But, says his daughter, they certainly did not grow in the hedgerow and they were never yellow when they were picked in November - they were green and brown, mottled with crimson.

Now you know the truth about the D'Arcy spice apple. But just how did Dr. Salter come to get that father of them all? That is a riddle wrapped in a mystery inside an enigma - as Sir Winston Churchill once said - though not about the D'Arcy Spice.

LITTLE EASTON

We nibble our muesli and crunch through our bran flakes, eat our fruit and our poly-unsaturated margarine - and think how modern we are. But healthy food is not as modern an idea as you might think. There was a Food Reform Society trying to wean us off bacon and eggs and other evils a century ago.

It was Takeley's village constable, P.C. Everard who had the idea of calling a meeting to publicise the idea of healthy eating in 1909. Lady Warwick was asked to chair the meeting which was held in a marquee erected in the garden of her home, Easton Lodge. What she said in opening the meeting is as apposite today as it was then: "Those who in the present day live strenuous lives have to consider the best way of husbanding their forces and nourishing themselves with those foods which are most likely to tell for force. The question of food reform must be of the greatest interest to the busy man and woman who wants to know as little as possible about the difficulties of digestion ... The Food Reform Society is doing splendid work in the country by bringing before people the great necessity of knowing something about food values, in the same way as the medical and nursing professions have done good work in telling the people subject which, twenty-five years ago, it was about the anatomy of the human body - considered improper for a woman to speak upon."

The Chairman of the Society said the reason for trying to tackle this problem of `food reform' was that there was "a greater prevalence of disease in the country than was necessary." People were inclined to say their ancestors ate plenty of meat and if that was good enough for them it was good enough for their descendants; but, he said, particularly among the middle and lower classes there was too much meat eaten. Food reformers in all humility were seeking to introduce a healthy diet which could eliminate many of the awful diseases like tuberculosis.

Mrs. Aylmer Maude, from Great Baddow, gave the housewives' point of view. She said that food reform could be more economical and just as tasty as other forms of dieting, with far less trouble. Which proves yet again that there is nothing new under the sun.

INGATESTONE

Had you seen Major Hilder eighty years ago you could not have picked him out from the crowd as anybody special, though his military bearing would have told you of his profession. He lived in a biggish house, called Huskards, at Ingatestone with his wife and family, rich but unostentatious. Yet he was very special to hundreds of girls who lived in the drear and desolate Dockland area of east London.

Every year Major Hilder would get together with the Reverend E. A. Gardner of Canning Town to choose two hundred girls for a holiday in the garden at Huskards. Just one qualification governed their choice: none of the girls should have any other chance of a holiday away from her grim surroundings.

When the girls arrived by special train they found bell tents erected in what might be called a canvas village in the spacious gardens, with all the necessary blankets set out ready for immediate use. In other parts of the garden all kinds of amusements had been erected, including swings and merry-go-rounds. Such was the excitement that few girls got much sleep on the first night, but thereafter such was the pace and variety of the entertainment there was no problem about bedtime.

In the morning the girls enjoyed the novelty of washing and bedmaking all in the open air, and breakfast in the barn, with fresh farm produce they could not hope to see in Docklands. It gave them the energy and sparkle missing from the daily lives in London's deadly atmosphere. In Ingatestone's healthy ozone they splashed in the large swimming pool, sunbathed on the cool, green grass, joined together in physical training and separated into smaller groups to ramble all over the Essex countryside. They learned that essential art of domestic economy - doing the washing up, led by their own church leaders.

So this little community learned to live together, to help each other, and to enjoy themselves for a whole week without a care in the world. There may just be some very senior citizens still alive who bless the Hilders for that never-to-be-forgotten week's holiday away from 'The Smoke'. By 1933 Major Hilder had been promoted to Lieutenant-Colonel. Did anyone deserve promotion more?

FOULNESS

The Broomway runs across the Maplin Sands from Wakering Stairs to Fisherman's Head. It is a road through the sea you could well say, for it is completely and deeply covered at high tide. It got its name from the fact that in former days the course of this causeway was marked by posts with bundles of broom tied at the top to make them clearly visible to the many people who once journeyed along it. There is no doubt that it was purposefully built up by human hands centuries before the Romans made their landfall in Essex. Experts reckon that a primitive prehistoric tribe made this track about a half a mile out and parallel with the shore because the forest then was impenetrable and in this way they could extend their range along the coast for hunting and food gathering.

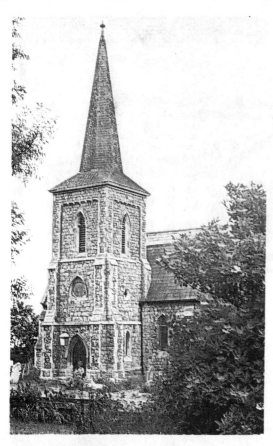

St Mary, Foulness

Can you imagine the excitement on 17th June, 1911, when 50 members of the Essex Field Club were driven in a convoy of big farm wagons all along the entire length of the Broomway. They did not chance the tide for the return journey, but took to the sea in a couple of sailing boats. The Broomway is rarely used now, the brooms have been battered down by the stormy seas, but it did come into its own again in 1953 when Foulness was inundated by the terrible floods, for it remained then as the only route by which people and animals could be evacuated. It would be best not to try negotiating it yourself, for since 1933 the War Department has taken over the whole island of Foulness, five miles long and two miles wide, and they would want to see your pass.

SOUTHEND

Eighty years ago the Southend Beauty Show at the Kursaal was practically a national event. Mr. Bacon, the manager, was very pleased to be able to report that within a few minutes of opening the doors every seat in the place was taken, by no less than over five thousand people. The paper reported, "The utmost order prevailed, and nothing marred the success of what was undoubtedly the greatest beauty show ever held in Southend." It was the first time a 'light chocolate lady' had applied to take part. Princess Dinovulu from Senegal did not take no for an answer - she insisted that she be allowed to compete - there was no rule against it - and she won the hearts of the crowd. Even

It would be a very chancy business trying to cover all six miles of the track between one tide and the next, so paths snaked out to the Broomway at regular intervals. The old parish registers of Foulness record many a death by drowning of people who tried to walk the Broomway as the tide was rising. It even gets a mention in the famous Raphael Holinshed's *The Chronicles of England, Scotland and Ireland* of 1577, where it says that it is possible for a man to ride to Foulness fair, "If he be skilful of the Causeway."

73

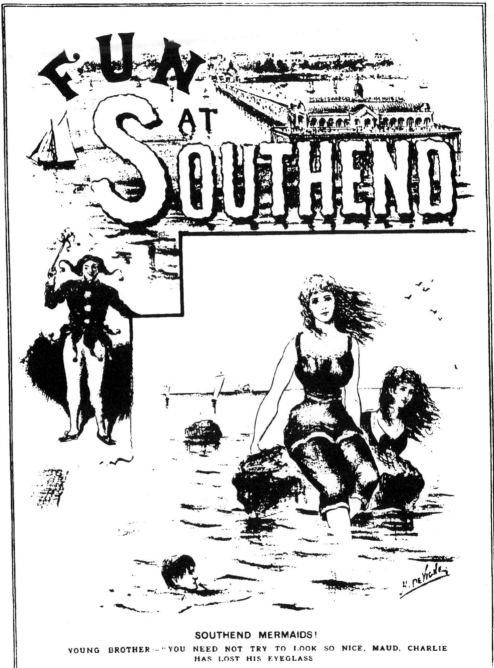

SOUTHEND MERMAIDS!
YOUNG BROTHER—"YOU NEED NOT TRY TO LOOK SO NICE, MAUD, CHARLIE
HAS LOST HIS EYEGLASS

if she could not hope to gain the votes of the judges, she so inspired one local poet, Claude Greening, that he wrote a poem in her praise and had it published in the paper. Here are the last three verses:

Cheerful, choc'late-coloured creature,
Compeer of the best,
Why should not your grace of feature
Triumph o'er the rest?

Dinovulu, damsel dusky,
Dressed in taste and style,
Many a throat will be quite husky
Cheering your sweet smile!

Buxom, bouncing, brilliant beauty,
Boasting lustrous eyes,
If Southend performs its duty
Yours must be the prize!

Prizes were awarded in three classes, according to hair colour, and on the length of the audience's applause for each contestant, timed on a stop watch.

It seems a shame to have to report that for all the poet's rhyming enthusiasm the charming Princess did not become a Queen.

COLCHESTER

On plaques and stones on various buildings in Colchester there is the name, time and again, of Viscount Cowdray, formerly Sir Wietman Dickinson Pearson. Until he was created a peer in 1910 and a Viscount in 1916, Sir Wietman had, for fifteen years, been the Member of Parliament for the Colchester Division. In 1910 he was also appointed High Steward

of Colchester. He it was who bought Colchester Castle, saving it from development, and presented it to the town. Some years later he purchased the house and estate of Holly Trees mansion and vested it in the ownership of the Borough, so that it might add to the Castle more space for the improved provision of museum facilities. When he heard that the Moot Hall needed an organ he was pleased again to help with the cost. He also paid for the crescent by the war memorial which was named after him as Cowdray Crescent, and, unostentatiously he was a great benefactor of the Essex County Hospital. Small wonder, then, that he was made a Freeman of the Borough in 1919. Viscountess Cowdray was accorded the same honour in 1922 and she succeeded her husband as High Steward in 1927.

Lord Cowdray, grandson of the founder of the engineering firm of S. Pearson and Company, was born in 1856. He started as an apprentice under his grandfather, worked his way through the ranks and made his money from oil. He introduced the revolutionary idea of filling oil tankers at sea through flexible pipes. Under him the company expanded, working on huge development contracts in Mexico, including drainage, water supply, harbours, railways and electrical installations. In the process it acquired vast tracts of land rich in oil. That same company built the Blackwall Tunnel under the Thames and extended Dover Harbour.

As Colchester's Liberal Member of Parliament he held his seat from 1895 until he took his seat in the House of Lords. Let the last words be with the *Colchester*

Colchester Castle, 1900

Gazette of 1956: "Nowadays, visitors wandering the Castle Museum may stop to wonder how the town came to own it. When they are told they will hear the story of a generous man who was also a pioneer in making available one of the world's major resources."

BRADWELL ON SEA

There is a place in Essex where the past meets the present in glorious seaside solitude. Go to Bradwell-on-Sea, take the road that heads towards Eastlands, park the car and walk the half-mile or so to St. Peter's Chapel. You are walking into history. This was the first church ever built on Essex soil. That was after St. Cedd landed here in about 657 to start his great campaign to convert the Saxons to Christianity and built this Church astride

St Peter ad Murum
Courtesy Essex County Council

76

the gateway in the crumbling walls of Othona, one of the Roman 'Forts of the Saxon Shore', with walls twelve feet thick and about 500 feet long. St. Cedd chose a good spot for his church for that old Roman fort had stoutly defied the ravages of the North Sea for ages and it had certainly deterred raiding Norsemen. The fort has all gone, robbed for other buildings and partly swallowed by the sea but that tiny church stands there still, though its chancel, in the form of an apse and the porch at the west end were lost in antiquity. The nave was demoted to use as a kind of lighthouse, then as a farmer's barn until, in 1920, its full significance was recognised and it was duly reconsecrated. This was due to the generosity of an unknown benefactor, an Essex man, who paid for the work needed to make it structurally sound while adding nothing that could be interpreted as 'restoration'. The first Bishop of Chelmsford conducted the service of reconsecration on 22nd June, 1920, and his successors have made the tiny church the subject of an annual pilgrimage.

Stroll along the beach and scuffle the sand with your feet; you will find it is not made of ground-down rock but of millions upon millions of sea shells reduced to powder by the ceaseless fretting of the waves. Look northeast as you wander on and you will see the great grey bulk of the Bradwell nuclear power station - a brooding gentle giant which has been providing electricity since 1963. Then look back at the church - in one glance you will have covered 1,300 years.

BEAUCHAMP RODING

If ever you are driving through the Roding villages look for the lane off the B184 which takes you through Beauchamp Roding to a driveway of a house called Hornets. In the corner where the drive meets the lane you will see the tombstones of a farmer and his family, now deep in brambles and nettles. That farmer was Isaac Mead.

Born in January, 1859, at a cottage in High Easter his strength of character was shown when he was only nine years old. Overhearing his parents discussing their desperate financial plight one night, he

The tombstone of Susan Mead

77

slipped out of the cottage, ran over to the Bury Farm bailiff and asked him for a job as from the next Monday. He was, of course, steered gently back home. But he was only eleven years old when he left school and started work in earnest, minding sheep, cutting thistles and milking cows, from dawn to dusk for just half a crown (12½p) a week. At thirteen he fell out of a tree he was shaking to bring down acorns for the pigs, and broke his thigh. Medical treatment then was primitive - he spent two months in a splint which sandwiched his whole leg. The day it was removed his mother helped him outside to sit in the sunshine. He was so weak that he fainted, fell out of the chair, and broke that thigh again. This time the splints went from his armpit and stretched beyond his foot. What a lesson he learned in patience and perseverance.

In his late teens he took a job in a windmill and learned the whole craft of the miller. His quick-thinking saved the mill when a sudden storm blew up which wrecked the mill at neighbouring White Roding. In 1882 he married Susan Smith and took the final big step to independence, renting Waples Mill Farm at Beauchamp Roding. He had this corner of the field consecrated by the Bishop so that he and his family might be buried in the land which had supported them in life. In 1923, when he was 64, he wrote his autobiography, called *Life Story of an Essex Lad*. In his foreword the Reverend Edward Gepp says, "Mr. Mead is a successful man. Risen from the lowest grade of farm labour, he has, by strenuous and intelligent exertion, become farmer, master miller, and owner of land..." And so a whole life is circumscribed in a simple epitaph.

Isaac Mead
at Waples Mill Farm,
Beauchamp Roding

CHIGNALL ST JAMES

Way up the Chignall road in Chelmsford a signpost points left to Chignall St. James. Near that junction, on the left-hand side stands a church, a 'tin tabernacle' in green corrugated iron. If only those green walls could speak they would tell you this story:

In 1923 a lady lived in Poplar Villa, hard by the church. She was just a humble housewife, and she was as surprised as any one of us would be when she felt, or rather heard, that God was speaking to her, wanting to use her. She went to her Bible, opened it at random and at once her eyes fell on the words: "Suffer the little children to come unto me ..." and she understood that she must start a Sunday School in the village. She found the courage to talk to children as they passed by, to welcome them into her home. She got pictures and books for them to look at and she told them stories from the Bible. Soon up to thirty children were attending regularly at what could now be called a Sunday School. Through the children she met the parents and discovered that they, too, were longing for a place to meet and talk and pray together.

So Mrs. Whybrow, that inspired Sunday School teacher, persuaded the bailiff at Brick Barns Farm, just up the road, owned by the Marriage family, to let her have one of his rooms for a weekly adult meeting. Through the following winter the meeting grew in numbers and in purpose - the room was overflowing. Then the Lord, through another random opening of the Bible, spoke again, in the words of Haggai, "Go up to the mountain and bring wood and build the house ..." But a building needs a site; it took a lot of enquiry and persistence before, on 1st January, 1926, Mrs. Whybrow obtained permission from Mr. Llewellyn Marriage to build the church on that corner of his land near her house.

"Bethel was officially opened - built by faith and prayer at the cost of £185 - completely free of debt." - I quote from the programme of a social gathering held on 24th January, 1967, to mark the retirement of Mr. and Mrs. Whybrow as Superintendents of the church. Their monument is that very church, still standing brave and welcoming.

TILBURY

I have recounted some strange stories in my strolls down memory lane, some from days not so long ago. Here is one that people in their eighties might well remember. All I ask you to do is to sharpen up your imagination and come with me down to Tilbury of 29th December, 1925.

In all the hustle and bustle of the busy cargo and passenger port as it then was, we must look for the big steamer *Clan Urquhart* which has just come in. It has tied up, its passengers have just gone ashore, and now the dockers have taken over, to unload its cargo, which includes at the end of this trip a very unusual consignment - a whole collection of animals destined for an English zoo. They have come all the way from Africa to the dreary desolation of a wintry Essex

Birdseye view of the East & West India Dock Extension at Tilbury

dockside where the River Thames swirls cold and forbidding.

At this moment an ostrich takes the stage in its own little drama. It does not like being hauled out of the hold in its own special packing crate; it kicks out as only an ostrich can, smashes the side of the crate and falls from a great height into that icy river. Now, you should know that all the animals had been sent in the care of an Egyptian keeper, one Mustafa Marmot, a most unlikely name for a hero. Yet hero he was, for, on seeing the ostrich surface in a cloud of spray, the brave fellow promptly dived off the ship's rail to rescue his benighted bird.

Already the great bird was swimming away with its long legs flailing like paddlewheels, and the current was taking it and Mustafa out into midstream. Quick-witted dockers had sized up the situation; they grabbed ropes and threw them far out to where Mustafa could grab a couple. He held on to one and managed to pass the other round the ostrich in such a way that they both could be dragged back to the quayside. The ostrich seemed none the worse for its immersion so, after a good rub down it was placed in a cage and made ready for onward transit. Mustafa was hauled aboard, wrapped in blankets and taken down to the Captain's cabin for hot drinks and warm congratulations.

BORLEY

Borley is a village in that beautiful rolling countryside on the border with Suffolk, looking down on the valley of the Stour. Its church has three unusual points - the first is the topiary which borders the church path, the second is the nave which experts date to shortly after the Battle of Hastings, and the third is that this little church has no patron saint. Perhaps that is what caused the first little riffle of superstition which led to the old rectory, built in 1863, becoming known as 'The Most Haunted House in England'.

It all started with the old legend, concocted, maybe, by some farm labourer to entertain his fellow tipplers at a celebration of 'harvest home', that a monk and a nun, caught eloping from a monastery and convent on this site, were caught and summarily put to death. Their spirits continued to haunt the place in the long black nights of those power-less days, and other spirits were added for good measure, including an unaccountable coach driven by a headless coachman.

The rectory became world news in June, 1929, when the Rector wrote to the *Daily Mirror* of these weird manifestations. They brought in Harry Price the well-known psychical researcher and journalist, who seemed to set off even more violent manifestations of unquiet spirits. The Rector regretted his action - he left, and the rectory stayed empty for six months. Strangely enough, in that period no spiritual activity was observed, but when the new Rector and his wife, the Foysters, came to live there in 1930 the weird spirit writing on the walls and the poltergeist activity brought a resurgence of world-wide publicity - until saner counsels prevailed. The Rector's wife came under suspicion, and after an exorcism by local spiritualists all that day and night activity by the unhappy ghosts ceased abruptly.

Price rented the Rectory himself for a year from 1937 and had forty-eight 'investigators' keeping watch there through many a black night. He could draw no firm conclusion from the scanty evidence.

At midnight on 27th February, 1939, the rectory was burnt down. The remains were sold to make wartime aerodromes, yet still sensation seekers make it a place a pilgrimage.

BURNHAM ON CROUCH

How wonderful it must have been before the Second World War when, if you had the cash, you could fly in almost complete freedom - and get the back-up service which would make today's earthbound motorists green with envy. Look what happened in Essex on a summer's day in August, 1932. A 'machine' as they liked to call it then, a two-seater de Havilland Puss-Moth monoplane, took off from Pevensey, in Sussex, piloted by Lieutenant Commander Geoffrey Rodd who had with him a rather mysterious, un-named lady passenger.

In taking off, however, the tail and the rear wheel were damaged, and rendered his intention to land with the lady on the Sussex downs unsafe and impractical. He needed help so he headed for Rochford aerodrome or a flat landing place as near it as possible.Time and fuel were running low when, a bit off course, he appeared over Burnham, where the good folk, out for an afternoon's stroll heard the strange noise in the sky and watched the still stranger sight of the 'plane circling lower and lower to make a perfect landing, despite its damage, on the smooth and level lawns of the recreation ground. That was at three o'clock.

The pilot went off to the Royal Corinthian Yacht Club to telephone to Rochford for an engineer to come over and repair the plane, while the lady had to endure the gaze of a great crowd of adults and children who quickly gathered round this interesting machine. The engineer came over from Rochford in a bi-plane, arriving before the pilot could get back from the telephone. He had brought spares with him and in half an hour or so he had refitted the wheel and repaired the damaged skin.

While Lt. Cmdr. Rodd's machine was still grounded another monoplane circled round and tried to effect a landing. It skimmed the ground, struck a ridge of earth and was shot up so high that, apparently the pilot decided discretion was the better part of valour. He scribbled a note, descended again and threw it out for our hero to read. As he flew away again the big crowd which had gathered were thrilled to watch him skim the telegraph wires and the house-tops in Station Road in dashing fashion. By half-past six Lt. Cmdr. Rodd and the Rochford engineer took off together. Never before had such a sight been seen in Burnham.

SILVER END

Silver End, once a small hamlet in the parish of Rivenhall, two miles north of Witham and eight south-east of Braintree, is entered in the last county directory published by Kelly's as, "A model village." Its churches, conformist and non-conformist, were not built until 1930. The houses were all built in the late 'twenties. It was a very special place seventy-five years ago.

It is not often we hear of a man setting up a business like Francis Crittall did with his metal window factory in Braintree and then going on to build a special village to house all his workers in a branch of those works out in the countryside where special accommodation was planned to house men disabled in the Great War. By 1926 the village was `up and running' as we might say these days, though the churches were to follow. It is only recently that I was able to get a word-of-mouth account of just what `the Guv'nor' Francis Crittall did, and how much of a village `feel' he had engendered in the new community of Silver End.

It was just before Christmas, 1938, when the doctor, R. M. Martin, had the idea of a children's party to which every child in the village would be invited - a `Monster New Year's Eve Party' held in the specially built village hall. For five weeks every kind of club and organisation in the village was roped in to make its contribution. One bought the presents, another undertook the decorations, a third organised the entertainment, the music and the dancing. Yet another group of volunteers put in hand twenty-six 'side-shows' which filled the six rooms of the hall. Refreshments were planned - enough to feed an army.

Though Crittall's had guaranteed the organisers against any loss they were not called on so to do because the whole village worked so well together in house-to-house collection that there was money enough and to spare. Straight after lunch on the great day no less than 375 children under fourteen turned up. Father Christmas, in the jovial shape of Mr. H. W. Abercrombie, gave every one of them a present. Punch and Judy and comic turns and conjuring followed in quick succession. Tea and drinks were dispensed by willing helpers, followed by further entertainment including the community singing of popular songs. During the course of all this merrymaking 'Young Mr. Crittall' called in to wish everyone well. What a happy memory for people who are pensioners now.

Chelmsford from the air, 1920. *Photograph by Fred Spalding*

CHELMSFORD

A couple of generations have grown up taking television totally for granted. They got their pictures bounced off a satellite and switch from channel to channel from the depths of a comfortable armchair, but few viewers realise how much Essex men contributed to the introduction of this marvellous invention more than sixty years ago.

The *Burnham Advertiser* in September, 1932, told us: "Mr. Roland J. Kemp, of Tillingham, is making a name for himself in the `wireless' world. After leaving school Mr. Kemp went to the Marconi Works at Chelmsford, where he now holds a responsible position. He is closely associated with the new Marconi television marvel, which created a sensation at the meeting of the British Association at York a few days ago. With two others he has been experimenting for two years on this wonderful invention, their plans having been inspected from time to time by Senatore Marconi, who has added his suggestions."

The *News Chronicle* at that time declared, "Messages typewritten in London can be read immediately on a screen thousands of miles away ... business men may soon expect to see world prices flashed on a screen on their office walls, news may be transmitted silently on home television sets, and Scotland Yard will be able to catch more criminals."

A local paper proudly proclaims: "Mr. Kemp was in charge of a machine at York which received a message from Chelmsford, spelling itself out on the screen. It is possible by this process to televise letters from one inch to a foot in height on to a screen thousands of miles away at the rate of 60 to 120 words a minute."

It seems a pity that, neither in Essex in general or Chelmsford in particular has there been established a museum to mark the origins of world-shrinking radio and television in this part of the world. What an important place Essex holds in this amazing history of technical innovation and development.

UPMINSTER

Essex is famous for so many things that it is not surprising that one grisly `first' is conveniently forgotten. It was in the air over our county that the first double suicide from an aeroplane took place, on 21st February, 1935.

Elizabeth, 23, and Jane, 20, were daughters of Mr. Coert Du Bois, the American Consul General at Naples. While staying there the girls got to know a couple of handsome English pilots - Flight Lieutenant Beatty and Flying Officer Forbes. Within ten days Jane was hopelessly in love with the latter. Then, while the girls were in Paris, came the awful news that a British flying boat had crashed at Messina and both officers were killed. Jane was inconsolable.

The two girls were both sensitive and excitable. Elizabeth was always ready to give way to Jane's influence, indulging her because she was what was then termed `sickly'. So it was that Jane persuaded her sister to join her in a desperate plan. They flew to London in a Hillman six-seater airliner on a commercial flight, stayed in a hotel for a few days, then chartered a similar plane to fly just the two of them from the airfield at Abridge to Paris, piloted by the same man who had brought them over. To head off any suspicion they had told the company that there were to be six passengers, then at the airfield they said their four friends had cried off at the last moment. So up they went and in a few minutes they were looking down on Gidea Park from over two thousand feet.

The pilot had left open the flap between the cockpit and the cabin, but one of the girls asked him to close it because of the draught. Now he could not see his passengers. Over Upminster the sisters opened the cabin door and, locked in each other's arms, they plunged down to their terrible death together. The pilot had a terrible shock when he opened the flap again to find that his passengers had, literally, disappeared into thin air. At the inquest the Coroner told the jury that it was obvious that the girls "were not in a right state of mind" when they jumped, so the verdict was brought in -" Suicide while of unsound mind."

A staff outing from Hillman's in 1932

GALLEYWOOD

Galleywood Common, south of Chelmsford, is a lovely open space where you can park the car, have picnics, fly kites or just walk about the woody greenery. Had you been driving down the Stock road at that spot in 1935 you would have had to wait, on race days, while the horses galloped down the hill, round across the road and back up again to the finish under the eyes of hundreds of spectators in the grandstand which was built in 1890 when the course was altered. Racing

Galleywood Race-course, 1930

started here some two hundred and fifty years ago and was recognised by George III who gave two prizes worth a hundred guineas each to be raced for.

That grandstand incorporated a public house called The Admiral Rous, after the famous horse-racing admiral who had it built originally as his own private grandstand. This is where Samuel Crozier comes into the picture. He was a publican who once kept the Globe at Rainsford End in Chelmsford. His first wife died in a mental hospital; then he met Cecilia, barmaid at the Fleece in Duke Street, Chelmsford. He was then unemployed but together they put in for the licence of the Admiral Rous, obviously a good little earner on race days.

But Crozier was already addicted to the bottle and his drinking bouts made him aggressive and very cruel. After the pub was closed at night there was no-one living near enough to hear the rows. Cecilia had nowhere else to go. The customers saw the evidence of the beatings Crozier inflicted. After months of such treatment she was reduced to a shadow of her former cheerful self. As a woman too weak to offer resistance she was the target for the drunken bully's violence. One night he went too far, and threw Cecilia down on the floor so hard that she struck her head against it and never got up again.

Crozier was apprehended, tried and sentenced to death. He was hanged in Chelmsford prison on 5th December, 1899, to get his place in history as the last man to be hanged in Chelmsford.

BRAINTREE

What a field day the newspapers had back in September, 1936, covering the great lion hunt at Braintree. It was on Wednesday, 23rd September, that the circus came up from Maldon and pitched its big top in Usher's meadow, Braintree, off the Coggeshall road. At half past ten in the morning the lion's cage was being opened for a cleaner, and just a moment's inattention allowed the lions the chance to leap to their freedom.

They immediately savaged one of the circus horses, which later had to be shot, then they rushed across the field and into the gardens of adjoining houses In no time at all they had killed two of Mrs. Joslin's Rhode Island pullets, leaving their mangled remains in their wake. News of the escape flashed round the town and, believe it or not, people flocked to the field to see the lion hunt. Fortunately, a couple were quickly tracked and re-captured by the keepers, but the other two were a problem. Mr. Witard, a seventy-year-old living at Alberta House met one of them face to face: "On walking through an open gate on to my lawn I was greatly surprised to see a huge lion standing there within a few feet of me...I raised my arms and called out, 'Get back'. He didn't attempt to attack me, but went back a few paces." Mr. Witard warned his wife and daughter not to go out by the back door. Just as well, for the lion had walked through it and into the kitchen. Brave Mr. Witard shouted at it again - and it backed out again. It was not until it was all over that the old man nearly died of shock.

Mrs. Joslin had the biggest fright. She had left her four-month-old baby in its pram outside her back door - and saw a large lion rush up her garden path and leap clear over that pram. She showed terrific courage in dashing out, grabbing the baby and rushing back in to slam the door tight shut. In another house Mrs. Cox had taken her little girl with her to neighbour Mr. Hurry for safety and reassurance. They were looking out of a back bedroom window when they saw a lion bound up to the dining room, utter a dreadful roar, and leap right through its window. For a whole hour it stood in that room, roaring and snarling, then it went into the scullery and jumped out of that window, breaking down the sink in its progress,

The keeper appeared in the nick of time and lured the lions back to their cage. That baby could still be alive and claiming he or she is the only person to be run over by a lion.

COGGESHALL

Looking at the church of St. Peter-ad-Vincula at Coggeshall today you would not believe that it had been almost demolished by a land-mine back in 1940. By 1956 it had been rebuilt exactly as it had looked before the war and it is now impossible to distinguish the parts which had to be replaced. The dear old man who was the verger in the wartime days told a very strange story.

A week or so before the bombing he had seen German planes flying high above the church as if they were on a reconnaissance mission. Then, a few days later he was going to the church to do his duty at early morning communion and looked up at the sky to size up the weather to come when, to his utter astonishment he saw a plane using smoke, as he put it, to draw a huge swastika in the sky. He was sure this was some kind of omen, but of what he could not guess. He found out all too sadly what it meant five days later when that vicious land-mine floated down to explode in the churchyard.

The stout tower built five hundred years ago stood up to the explosion and the blast but its roof was blown off, so the bells were lowered to the floor of the nave and a great deal of temporary repair was carried out in order that worship could continue. In those days the lack of labour and materials and the necessity to put damage to houses at the top of the list of priorities meant that it was not until after 1945 that restoration work could be put in hand. In the meantime strong winds and rain caused the upper works of the tower to fall in, causing as much damage as the land-mine itself. Tourists today who admire the old church in its beautiful setting can have no idea of how the good folk of Coggeshall suffered that night of the bombing.

The monument that everybody looks for in the church is the one on the wall of the sacristy to Mrs. Mary Honywood, who brought up a family of sixteen children at neighbouring Marks Hall, now demolished. Those children each had very large families and so did the grandchildren, so that, while she was still living at the age of 93, she could claim to have no less than 367 descendants - what a headache for genealogists.

St Peter-ad-Vincula,
Coggeshall

BURNHAM ON CROUCH

There were many heroes in the last war, from those dashing fighter pilots who fought enemy bombers in the sky to the innocent, unarmed housewives who dragged their wounded neighbours from the ruins of their bomb-torn homes; from soldiers suffering onslaughts in foreign lands to sailors squashed like sardines in ships under horrific bombardment. There were people, too, caught up in war who had no time to be heroes, had no defence against attack.They were the men of the Merchant Navy, and I would like to tell a story of just two such human beings whose names should be added to the roll of reluctant heroes - a man and a boy.

Harry Eves and his son Adam were doing their job and nothing more - the job they did every day - sailing their barge along the coast taking anything that anybody wanted carrying from port to port. At eight o'clock on a fine but chilly morning in March, 1943, they had roused early, got the good ship *A laric* properly stowed and ready for sea, and hoisted the great browny-red sails to stand out from Burnham with the tide, bound for Felixstowe. They had eaten their breakfast, and with their little cocker spaniel sitting up on deck enjoying the gentle rhythm of the ocean they were making good time in friendly weather and a moderate sea.

Then a buzzing noise quickly turned to a shattering roar as six fighter planes flew over yellow noses gleaming. Harry and Adam gave them a wave, thought they were `ours'. They were so wrong. Those planes disappeared over the horizon, only to reappear in seconds. Roaring low they shot the old *A laric* through and through with machine-gun and canon fire. Harry, at the tiller, was the most susceptible to the withering fire. He was wounded all over his body, collapsed on the deck, and minutes after, in a horrible, eerie silence with the planes long across the horizon, he died in his son's arms. Miraculously Adam was no more than scratched. Bravely he did what he could for his father, then he swung the tiller round to head for help in Burnham.

But, such is the fellowship of the sea, help came quickly from all the ships in the vicinity which had heard the dreaded sound of gunfire, though nothing could save his Dad. What about the dog? - Well, it had two bullets pass through the same hole in one ear, and survived to bark its own defiance.

LANGHAM

Langham lies on the bank of the Stour, the river which marks the boundary between Essex and its northern neighbour Suffolk, and six miles northeast of Colchester. Its church, dedicated to St. Mary, was built in Saxon times, but well-intentioned Victorian restoration and a dreadful fire in the tower in 1879 have obscured its antiquity. The ancient peace of the place is as enjoyable as it was when John Constable, that famous painter we can claim as an Essex artist, climbed up the steps to the top of the tower some two hundred years ago to make sketches for his celebrated view of Dedham Vale.

He was born too soon for one of the beauties of Langham - the apple orchards which in spring froth pink and white with blossom. In those orchards there is one apple in particular which had not even been 'invented', if that is the right word, until 1950 or thereabouts. It happened like this; George Dummer lived in Langham and loved gardening. He had a good vegetable and fruit plot in which one day he found a seedling apple tree which had come up quite by chance. He nurtured it till it fruited, and it rewarded him by producing a new red and yellow apple which ripened much earlier than any other variety, and tasted delicious.

Delighted, George called it Dummer's Pride and grew more. The big fruit farmers and merchants went for it in a big way, for it was the season's first English apple to go on sale and was bound to be a commercial success. But they did not like the name - not commercially attractive they said - so somebody came up with the brilliant idea of calling it 'Discovery'. That was in 1961; now the trees are grown in their thousands and the apples are eaten in their millions. They should have called it Langham Discovery, for it is giving the Worcester Pearmain a run for its money, and the world should know that this juicy red-and-yellow first of the season's apples comes from good old Essex. What a refreshing snack it would have made for cheerful, friendly John Constable as he worked away up there on the church tower.

Woodham Ferrers station, 1911.
Maldon lies straight ahead, the line to Southminster branches to the right